Thanks for your interest,

Rudi Zunderman

Justice in the Jungle
Copyright © 2021 by Paul Zonderman
NORTHUMBERLAND PRESS, NISKAYUNA, NEW YORK

This is a memoir. It reflects the author's present recollections of experiences over a period of years. Certain names, locations, and identifying characteristics have been changed, and certain individuals are composites. Dialogue and events have been recreated from memory and, in some cases, have been compressed to convey the substance of what was said or what occurred.

All rights reserved. No part of this book may be used or reproduced in any form, electronic or mechanical, including photocopying, recording, or scanning into any information storage and retrieval system, without written permission from the author except in the case of brief quotation embodied in critical articles and reviews.

Book design by Jessika Hazelton
Printed in the United States of America
The Troy Book Makers • Troy, New York • thetroybookmakers.com

To order additional copies of this title,
contact your favorite local bookstore
or visit www.shoptbmbooks.com

ISBN: 978-1-61468-686-6

JUSTICE IN THE JUNGLE

PAUL ZONDERMAN

NORTHUMBERLAND PRESS
NISKAYUNA, NEW YORK

DEDICATION

I lovingly dedicate this book to my wife Ann of 57 years, who lived with me on MCB Quantico, Virginia and MCB 29 Palms, California, and kept the home fires burning while I spent my last year of service in Vietnam. She was a real "trooper" and has always stood by my side. She encouraged me to write this book. And to my children, Lauren, Jeffrey and Kyra, and grandchildren, Bella and Claire, I leave this book as my legacy. Let them go forth in life with pride and remember the Latin motto:

"Omnia mea mecum porto" - All of me I carry with me.

2021

ANN AND PAUL

LAUREN

BELLA, CLAIRE, KYRA, JEFF

ACKNOWLEDGMENTS

Many thanks to: my family, Ann, Lauren, Jeffrey, and brother, Richard, for always believing, and to Eleanor and Jesse Aronstein, Annette and Roger Keen, and Dee and Frank Wind, my first readers. Together their incisive and generous feedback encouraged and guided me. And to every family member and friend over the years who has listened to me tell my stories, thank you for your understanding and support.

CONTENTS

INTRODUCTION 1
ONE: **IN THE BEGINNING** 3
TWO: **LEAVING BOSTON FOR CALIFORNIA** 7
THREE: **THE LONG FLIGHT TO OKINAWA** 15
FOUR: **ON THE GROUND IN VIETNAM** 19
FIVE: **LEARNING THE ROPES** 33
SIX: **WELCOME TO PHU BAI** 39
SEVEN: **ROUTINE DUTIES** 47
EIGHT: **A LETTER TO MY DAD** 55
NINE: **THE GIBSON TRIAL** 61
TEN: **TALKING POLITICS** 87
ELEVEN: **THE RED CROSS** 95
TWELVE: **REST AND RECUPERATION (R & R)** 99
THIRTEEN: **THE CHARLES WOODLEY TRIAL** 105
FOURTEEN: **LUNCHEON SURPRISE** 111
FIFTEEN: **BUFFALO DAY** 115
SIXTEEN: **THE BARDACK TRIAL** 117
SEVENTEEN: **FAREWELL TO WAR** 121
EIGHTEEN: **WHO AM I?** 125
EPILOG 129
AGENT ORANGE 133
"THE PEOPLE VS. AGENT ORANGE" 137
NEGATIVE POPULARITY 141

INTRODUCTION

This book is intended to be a non-fictional narrative, based upon truth and my memories originated over fifty years ago which I believe are accurate. The names given to the characters and the military units involved are fiction. Dialog is not always in the King's English, but in the language of the people in country.

My grandfather, Bernard Appel, served in the Spanish American War. My father, Bernard Zonderman, was a major in the Army Medical Corps in World War II. I was seven years old when he completed his service. As a Captain in the Marine Corps, I am the third generation in my family to have served in the U.S. armed forces. I have written my stories, in this limited edition, intended for the reading of my family and friends.

BERNARD APPEL
SPANISH-AMERICAN WAR

BERNARD ZONDERMAN
MAJOR, ARMY MC, WWII

PAUL ZONDERMAN
CAPTAIN, USMC, VIETNAM

ONE

IN THE BEGINNING

I had enlisted in the Marine Corps in 1961, during my senior year in college. I also had decided that I wanted to be an attorney. When I discussed this with the recruiters, they told me I could be in the Platoon Leaders Class (PLC) Law Program. They would let me finish my first year of law school, spend the summer twelve weeks in the "PLC" training, become commissioned as a 2nd Lieutenant, and remain in the inactive reserve status as I completed the last two years of law school. I'd have to maintain passing grades at law school, and then have one chance to pass the Massachusetts Bar Exam. Otherwise, I owed the Marine Corps three years of active duty. I took the Oath, became a Marine Officer at age 23, and then completed law school over the next two years. I graduated from an Ivy League law school in 1964, passed the Massachusetts Bar Exam, and married Ann, my childhood sweetheart, in August of that year.

Active service began in January of 1965, at age 25. I completed a short course in Newport, Rhode Island, at the Navy School of Justice, and then Ann and I drove to Quantico, Virginia, where I began the intense six months of Officer's Basic School. We took an apartment in a nearby town. It was here at Quantico that I received the full infantry officers' rugged training. At the end of Basic School, I was assigned to my first duty station, and I had been given the MOS (Military Occupational Specialty) of "Trial/Defense Counsel Officer in General Courts Martial" (4405). I was assigned to the Marine Corps Base at 29 Palms, California, in the Mojave Desert, and we took an enjoyable scenic drive across the United States.

When we first arrived at 29 Palms, we were a bit skeptical about living in the Mojave Desert. It was hot, flat, empty, and desolate. The base was like a small oasis nestled at the foothills of mountains. We had a nice little air-conditioned house in the officers' quarters area.

For part of the time there, I served as the Base Headquarters Company Adjutant. My additional duty was as the "Casualty Assistance Calls Officer," a stressful assignment. Vietnam was heating up now, and it was my duty to give families within a fifty-mile radius of the base, the first personal notice that their child had been killed. I took a Navy Chaplain with me, and we drove out in a marked military vehicle. It was a heartbreaking job which needs no discussion.

As I approached a few months short of the last thirteen months of a three- year enlistment, I was transferred into the Base Legal Office. One day, walking by my colonel's office, I was called in and told that I was going to Vietnam, to the 3rd Marine Division, Fleet Marine Forces. There was no humor in the colonel's soft blue eyes. He had simply told me directly what he had to tell me. "I got the word through channels. Your orders should be coming through in a couple of weeks." The colonel added that I would have thirty days to travel cross-country to Boston, my home of record, from where I would depart.

I walked into my own office and tried to settle my thoughts. I had seen many of my friends go. I knew many wives were living on the base while husbands were overseas. It was a fact of life, but now it was our life. I would be one of those men to have gone.

I then called to mind that early in that year, 1966, our first child had been born, held by both of us, and died two days later in a Navy Hospital. It was a crushing experience for us. We had a room and a crib all set up. I then had to dissemble it so there would be no reminders. I also had to quietly arrange for the baby to be sent to Boston for burial.

The noon break had come all too quickly, and it was time to go home for lunch. I didn't know where the time had gone. I remembered the day that Ann had jubilantly told me she was pregnant again. She was so happy. After the first tragedy, now I had to leave her to face the new childbirth alone. How shall I tell her? I was heartsick with the thought that she would be three months pregnant when we left for Boston and that she would give birth seven months into my thirteen months in Vietnam. She would have to face a double-barreled challenge. This would also mean that I wouldn't see my child until he/she was seven months old. I hoped that having our baby to love might help Ann through the months of sadness and loneliness and fear. It was morbid to also think about the possibility of my death. It was there. There was so much more at stake now.

The short ride to my base housing seemed quicker than usual. When I arrived, Ann knew almost immediately that something was wrong. This sensitivity which had always been so attractive, now had its drawbacks. I told her quickly just as I had been told. There was no other way to do it. Instantly she broke down and began crying hard. I would never forget my feeling of inadequacy. Look what I have done to this poor girl. She had the spirit to come and join me in the Marine Corps. She tolerated shooting the .45 in the desert. She was a good sport in learning to drive a small motorcycle. She had held herself together after the death of our first child. There was nothing I could say but "I love you, and we'll get through this."

It was natural to toy with the possibility that the orders were mistaken. Briefly and guiltily, I considered trying to get them changed based on hardship. I put that out of mind quickly. Although I had Ann and the baby to worry about, I could never live with myself if I tried to duck my duty and responsibility. No, I did not want Vietnam. I had not asked for it, but I was no different than anyone else. The war was not the sort of thing you either believed or disbelieved in. It was a fact, here and now. I was a

Marine officer charged with a duty to carry out. I enlisted voluntarily with the knowledge of what I might be called upon to do. I could never justify my running away from it now. Besides any attempt to avoid my orders was made virtually impossible for me because of my additional duty as the Casualty Assistance Calls Officer. How can you tell parents the worst news in their life, their child was dead, and then try to avoid the danger yourself? Now I could only pray that no one would ever have to make a casualty call to my family, and perhaps hope that someday, there would be no casualty calls at all. The drive cross-country was scenic and interesting, and helped to distract us from the reason for our trip.

TWO

LEAVING BOSTON FOR CALIFORNIA

I was at Logan Airport in Boston, standing with Ann and my parents. "Flight 390 nonstop to San Francisco is now boarding at gate 22." The empty sensation in the pit of my stomach, as well as the announcement, said to me that it was time to go. People around me were starting to pick up their baggage and move toward the gate. In my green service uniform with gleaming captain's bars, I felt and looked very formal and military. I hoped that there would not be a scene. None of us wanted that. We were all trying hard to avoid it. I embraced Ann, kissing her quickly. I knew she was fighting back the tears - - that it would be a tough year for her. Yet, Ann knew that I was always embarrassed by public displays of affection, particularly when I was in uniform. I had told her once that the Marine Guidebook had said "no" to public embracing while in uniform.

Besides, all our goodbyes had been said the night before. Any display of emotion now would cause them all to break down. I turned to my father. We shook hands, hesitated, and then kissed. My father held on to my hand a few seconds longer than was comfortable emotionally. He finally released his grip with the recognition that he had to let go. He appeared suddenly older but resigned to the fact that his son must do his duty, just as he had done in World War II so many years ago. I remembered the picture of my dad in his World War II uniform, holding me in his arms.

As I started to walk to the departure gate, my mother leaned forward for her embrace. Unobtrusively, she pushed something into my hand. I knew immediately that it was a 'Chai' (to life) medal. Neither of us spoke, partially because we didn't trust our voices, and partially because nothing needed to be said. The 'Chai' would be returned to her when I came home again.

I looked around for a second, trying to indelibly print the faces on my memory. It would be a long time before they would be seen again. For just another moment, I could appreciate the nearness and companionship of the people I loved so dearly. This appreciation was always the real nature of a goodbye.

Now is the time. I turned abruptly to board the plane. For months, my mind had been geared for this moment. Forward. It was time to look ahead. As I was ready to enter the plane, I paused and looked back once again. The family waved from the window of the terminal - - already far away. I lifted my hand and then turned and entered the plane.

Finding a vacant seat, I placed my small carry-on bag under it and sat down. Other passengers were busy getting settled. The plane taxied out to the runway and stopped. Then it started to move down the runway picking up speed as it went. Finally, the ride got smoother indicating that we were airborne. Looking from the window, the individual landmarks got smaller as the plane leveled off. I leaned back in my seat trying to do the same with my emotions. Already I seemed so far away from my family and the parting. I felt like an observer watching this all happen to someone else. Yet, at the same time, I could feel the throbs of emotion which my family carried in their hearts as they made their way through the crowd to their car.

As the jet turned toward its destination, I focused on the future which was uncertain. The parting was pushed into a corner of my mind. It was a moment in history filled with other memories. The contacts with everything familiar and dear were cutoff. The new challenges were yet to come. I was in the twilight zone, a limbo between past and future.

What lay ahead for me was vague, and uncertain. I could not conjure up a picture of what it would be like. This prevented me from launching myself into it. But I resolved silently, I would face whatever lay ahead. I would do what I must.

The preparation was there and expressed in the Latin phrase my parents often recited to me as I grew: *'Omnia mea mecum porto.'* **All of me, I carry with me.** I was the sum of all that had gone before. I was like a basket into which all the stimuli in my life had been placed. My experiences, everything that I had ever seen, heard, or been taught, were part of me now, to be drawn upon when needed. I believed that if the training and learning of my lifetime were worthwhile and strong, I would be strong. If I failed, I would be letting down those close to me, and myself as well. I felt confident I was prepared.

I tried again to focus upon what war would be like. Even without any firsthand frame of reference, there were many indications from my Marine Corps training. War is military. It is organization along military lines. It is tactics, weapons, map reading, logistics, all areas with which I had a great deal of familiarity. The Marine officer's training was rugged, extensive, and most comprehensive. A Marine officer was ready. I was confident of this. They made sure at Quantico.

I recalled the twelve weeks of Platoon Leaders Class (PLC) training in the summer of 1962. This had been a physical screening process which eliminated half of the class. Upon completion, my father and uncle had come down to Quantico to pin the golden bars of a 2nd Lieutenant on my uniform.

The six months of Officers' Basic School at Quantico followed two years later in 1965. It was there that the intensified and refined infantry training took place. Graduation from Basic School was the true achievement.

Yes, I knew I was ready. I recalled my training in the handling of weapons. As an officer, the .45 caliber pistol would be my primary weapon. I had become quite proficient in its use. I owned my own .45, and often had practiced with it out in the California desert. I had qualified as an "Expert" with this weapon, and I proudly wore the Expert's badge on my uniform. I wore the Sharpshooter badge for the M-14 rifle as well. But even beyond this, I'd been trained in the use of any weapon which any soldier might be required to handle. Basic School taught me not only as an artisan utilizing the tools of my trade, but also as an instructor who might be called upon to educate others who would serve with and under me.

Such training included even the most unlikely weapons. I recalled the flamethrower. It was certainly not an officer's weapon. I could remember them strapping on the harness with a heavy tank of gas onto my back. It was like trying to hold a fire hose just after the hydrant had been turned on. I held on tightly as the compressed fuel burst out of the tank through the tubing and spewed forth from the nozzle in a stream of flame, inescapable and deadly. It was disquieting that I might have to rely on these skills to protect myself soon. The fact that I would be able to do so was to some extent a source of comfort.

Probably the greatest benefit I had derived from my Basic School training in 1965 was the endurance and respect for my own abilities which had been instilled in me. Confidence and Leadership were the hallmarks of my training. Often the task, whether it was a hike on the Hill Trail, an obstacle course, a mock operation, or a jog, would seem impossible. But, pushed by my superiors and my own motivation, I always seemed able to make it. It created a deep respect in me for that hidden reservoir of ability which goes unnoticed if it remained untapped. I was trained to know that it was there, and to call upon it when necessary.

As I shifted in my seat and took care to preserve the crease in my trousers, I recalled the first 15-mile hike at Basic School. When I had returned home that evening, I could scarcely climb the one flight of stairs up to the small apartment Ann and I shared just off the base in Triangle, Virginia. I had felt like a 90-year-old man, with a lifetime of aches and pains. But, soon afterwards, it was a 25-mile hike. And two weeks later, a 40-mile overnight hike. I recalled staggering the last of those 40 miles with biting pains in my feet caused by the bleeding blisters. I had learned in Quantico that I could do much more than I had ever imagined. The trick to it was motivation -- triumph of spirit over body. When the instructors saw that the troops could not take another walking step, they would invariably give the command to run. If one could hate words, I hated the phrase "double-time, march." As I went from a walk to a run, I was sure that I would pass out. The technique of the sergeants was to make us run until two Marines had passed out and were loaded onto the two ambulances which followed us. My muscles ached and my lungs burned. Each step was so bad that when the order came to return to a walking pace, the walking was a pleasure. I felt that I could go on forever. One thing was certain, I would never quit. This type of experience built up confidence. That confidence was with me now as I flew to California, the first stop in my travel to Vietnam. The one element that still threatened was the vagaries of war. The simple matter of luck. No training could assist me here. It might simply be a matter of being in the wrong place at the wrong time - - a sniper's bullet or a mortar round. Nothing could be done about this element of chance. But, even here, the training might help to bring down the odds.

    As the large 4 engine jet flew westward, I wondered exactly what my duties would be. Although trained as an infantry line officer, they would use me in a legal capacity when required. My MOS was 4405, Trial and Defense Counsel Officer in General Court Martials. Certainly, I would be preparing and trying Court Martial cases as well as doing administrative jobs. I had learned about a few of these from Jim, a friend from my Basic School days. He was the only lawyer in his platoon to be sent directly to Vietnam from training. After receiving my orders, I had written to Jim who would be coming home just about the time I was due to arrive in country. I might even be his replacement. Jim had written me that my duties would be primarily legal. When not prosecuting or defending Court Marshall cases, there were certain other interesting and challenging administrative assignments that I could be called upon to undertake. The job of Foreign Claims Officer was one he had cautioned me to avoid if possible. Each Division had an officer lawyer assigned to that duty. In a nutshell, the Foreign Claims Officer investigated the non-combat related injuries to the person and property of the Vietnamese. I would file the claim and physically pay the amount determined by higher authority. Often this meant going out into the countryside, and a great deal of traveling off the beaten path. While the job was considered dangerous, they hadn't lost any lawyers yet. I had made a mental note to avoid this job if possible. Obviously, there was nothing I could do about it; it was just a matter of luck. If I was getting there when the old "FCO" was leaving, I might just get tagged with the job. Right now, there were too many other things about which to be concerned.

Another lawyer who returned to 29 Palms from Vietnam educated his brother lawyers about the overseas Court Martials when he had come to the legal office. Apparently, the caseload over there was heavy, and his superior legal officer had laid down the law to his defense counsels. They had been told in no uncertain terms not to make too many waves, and that the Washington DC Appeals Court did not write their fitness reports. Their superior officer in Vietnam did. There was inherent conflict of interest here. The Commanding General gave the Staff Legal Officer the responsibility to maintain discipline within the command. Yet, the interests of his subordinate defense counsel officers were opposed to this position in as much as they were often defending the alleged violators of discipline. I hoped I would not be faced with that type of conflict. But should the occasion ever arise, I felt confident that I would not succumb to 'command pressure.' As a defense counsel, my first loyalty, as always, had to be to my clients. I would do my best for them. The ethics of my profession required nothing less. I was warned that many career legal officers were more concerned about advancements and promotions than they were about a particular client. Besides, I was only in for three years and need not worry about being passed over for colonel.

I was awakened by the movement of the man sitting next to me. The seat belt sign was lit again. They were starting their descent into California. The first leg of my journey was over.

THREE

THE LONG FLIGHT TO OKINAWA

I stepped off the bus which I'd taken from the airport to Travis Air Force Base near San Francisco. I asked for directions to the Bachelor Officers' Quarters (BOQ) and checked in. It would probably be a couple of days before finding my name on a passenger list for a flight to Vietnam. Although in no hurry, it would be better if there was little delay. Waiting was always the worst part. For the next two days, I tried to keep myself busy sightseeing. A couple of times a day I would call into the flight departure section to see if I was booked for a flight. Finally, on the second morning, my name appeared on the passenger manifest for a flight leaving at 1:00 o'clock the following morning. I arranged to have my gear picked up and checked aboard. I made sure that I had not packed my dog tags. They were around my neck where they were supposed to be. I had gotten out of the habit of wearing them. Now I knew that they would be part of me for the next thirteen months. If there was one place where dog tags should be worn, that is in a combat zone.

At midnight, I walked over to the air terminal. After many cigarettes and much pacing, the word came to board. It was beginning. The flight to Okinawa would take me for final processing before moving on to Vietnam. Okinawa was in the neighborhood of my new duty station in Danang. It was a giant step toward Vietnam. As the plane took off, I looked down at the lights of San Francisco. It would be a long time before I would be seeing the States again.

Even though I had been a stranger in San Francisco, compared to where I was going, it seemed like home.

We were traveling on a large four-engine military jet transport. The thirteen-hour trip was uncomfortable and tiring. One can only sit for so long. I slept fitfully and woke up once when they passed out sandwiches and again when we landed to refuel briefly in Guam. Finally, we landed in Okinawa and deplaned in the hot sun. I was given a schedule of what we were supposed to be doing for the next three days. After drawing some blankets, linen, and a pillow, I sat on my bed and read the schedule.

As soon as I stepped out of the BOQ the next morning and first observed Okinawa in the daylight, I realized I was in a new and different land. Even though the base possessed all the physical attributes of bases anywhere, the Japanese lettering on the sides of miniature vehicles told me that I was on an island somewhere in Asia.

I first went to deposit my green uniform and cover in a storage building. I would not need them in Vietnam. They would get mildewed and ruined there. For the next thirteen months, all I would be wearing was boots and utilities. The storage facility was a big open warehouse run by a sergeant who provided a storage carton, writing my name and unit on the box. I imagined the day I would be back here picking up my uniform for the trip home.

That afternoon, I reported to the Infirmary where I would finish the inoculations begun in California. I was concerned about what I was being inoculated against, such as the Bubonic Plague. But if they had the plague where I was going, I sure as hell wanted to be inoculated against it. On the third morning my name appeared on a manifest. The flight would be leaving for Danang at 0200 hours. That evening I joined a group of Marines waiting out in front of the Mess Hall. Although there were several of them, each one felt alone. We made no real attempt to get acquainted since our union was only temporary. When the vehicles arrived for us, we threw our gear on the back of a truck and filed onto the bus to the airstrip. When we arrived at the Air Force departure area, I heard my name paged, and a sergeant handed me several papers. I was designated to be the Officer in Charge of the passengers. I was the senior officer on this flight to Vietnam. Should there be any delays or difficulties on the route, it would be my responsibility to take charge. I could just see the flight going down somewhere in the jungle with me leading these men as a tactical unit. Yes, I could see it all now: Zonderman's marauders running around the jungle raising cane with the enemy. Mercifully, I realized that it was a mere formality. Someone always had to be responsible. That was the military way.

We boarded the C-130, a four-engine propeller transport used in Vietnam. There were no customary seats inside. Rather we had webbed slings on which to sit. The men were jammed in. It seemed that the closer we got to Vietnam, the worse the flights were. Despite the discomfort and crowding, I fell asleep almost immediately.

From the maneuvering, I surmised we were preparing to land. There was nothing to be seen but clouds. As this was the monsoon season, the country was continually covered by a blanket of clouds. This coverlet was not penetrated until we were just above the airfield. As the aircraft plunged beneath the grayness, I got my first glimpse of Vietnam. My first thought was how rustic the country looked. Most notable was the lack of any tall structures. The plane was coming in over the South China Sea. Someone commented that the approach was always over the water. They tried to travel over land as little as possible. The planes also came in as steep as possible to lessen the likelihood of being hit by ground fire.

I could make out some shipping in the harbor and the South China seacoast. In the immediate area, there were patches of light-colored aluminum roofs. These would be the military complexes. The rice patties were simply low marsh lands separated into squares, like a green and brown patchwork quilt. I had seen pictures of them. The airfield at Danang was very busy. Many mean looking US fighter jets were spread around. The city of Danang was nearby with citizens and market places.

FOUR

ON THE GROUND IN VIETNAM

I stepped off the plane. I paused for a second as my boots hit the ground. I was in Vietnam. We milled around until our belongings were unloaded from the cargo section. We were standing on an air strip. The airport complex was huge. A variety of military planes were scattered about. The outer confines were ringed with barbed wire. The personnel who moved about with resignation all wore 'utilities' and carried weapons. Off in the distance I observed the rolling hills, with many building complexes nestled at their base.

There was no one there to tell us what to do. One might think that we would have been given some information regarding the procedure we were supposed to follow. I didn't want a brass band, but it would have been nice if someone were on hand to give us some instructions. This really amazed me. We had no orientation. There were no handouts to familiarize us with the area. We were standing in the drizzling rain, plunked down on an airfield on the other side of the world. But I was an officer, and in charge of the welfare of the passengers. As such, I would have to take the initiative. Looking around I spotted a building which seemed to be somewhat more prominent than the others. I started for it, dragging my footlocker and duffel bag behind me.

The rain was constant in the monsoon season. It was all very depressing. As I neared a small building, I saw a sign directing us to the transient facilities. I left my pile of gear and walked along the wooden catwalk toward one of the huts that seemed like the place to go. The men followed along, each man drifting toward the hut designated as his unit's reception station. I saw the sign designating the 3d Marine Division hut. I went in. The Warrant Officer behind the desk stood up as I entered. "I'm Captain Zonderman. I'm assigned to Division Legal." "May I have a copy of your orders, Sir?" I took out a copy of my orders and handed them to him. The Warrant Officer read them and endorsed the copy. He hesitated for a moment. I felt that he wasn't quite sure what to do with me. He probably had been used to just telling people to wait for a bus or truck. Realizing that I was an officer for Division Staff, he said that he would call and have me picked up. I thanked him and walked outside. Lighting up a cigarette, I gathered my thoughts. I didn't know what I had expected, but whatever it was, this was not it.

After about twenty minutes, a small military pickup truck pulled up in front of the shack. Captain Gus Anderson and a driver got out. They were covered with mud and looked weather-beaten. With their steel pots (helmets) and flak jackets, they looked the part of soldiers in a combat zone. As they approached, I sensed a hardness - - there were no smiles. I noticed that the captain was wearing only one boot. On the other foot, he had a sandal with a large dirty bandage wrapped around his foot. He was thin and gaunt and sported a thick mustache which dropped at the ends. When he hobbled up, I extended my hand. We introduced ourselves. The captain said that he had been sent to take me up to Division Legal Headquarters. I asked him what happened to his foot? With just the trace of a smile, he responded very casually that he had fallen into a punji pit[1]. It was not until a few days later, that I learned that he had only an ingrown toenail removed.

I climbed into the back of the truck. It was covered over with canvas, but open in the back, so I could see out. Captain Anderson

---

1 A Viet Cong trap. A hole in the ground filled with vertical pointed bamboo stakes, the top of which were coated with feces to expedite infection. The trap was covered over by foliage.

came around to the back and loaned me a steel pot, flak jacket, and a .45 pistol with a clip of ammunition. "Here", he said, "You may need this for the ride. This is pretty rough country." "Thanks," I said out loud. To myself I thought "Oh boy, here we go." I laid down in the back of the truck, leaning against my duffel bag. We started to ride through some very bushy countryside. All I really saw were some straw and bamboo huts and Vietnamese walking along the side of the road. They all looked very suspicious to me. The only signs of the military were an occasional truck or Jeep. The country seemed hostile and treacherous. I looked at the .45. I was not scared, just a little tense. A little later, I would find out that they had taken the long way around. The whole operation with a weapon and the "scenic route" was a standard bit pulled on all new officers. We were in a safe area of the base complex at Danang.

This was like the first day of anything. All was totally unfamiliar and therefore foreboding. I hoped that the time would pass quickly to the point that I knew the ropes. Once I understood what was going on, I would be more at ease.

After bumping along over the muddy dirt road for several minutes, we finally entered a military compound area built on a sloping hillside. When the truck stopped, I jumped out and sank into the mud. As I looked around, I saw simply constructed wooden huts built up on the side of the hill. Captain Anderson told me that they would find me a place to stay in one of these huts. I picked up my gear and followed along on the wooden catwalks which seemed to float on a sea of mud. After we found a vacant bed in one of the huts, Captain Anderson stated that an enlisted man would procure my bedding. I put my gear down next to the bed and looked around my new home. There were eight cots, four on each side. Some of the beds had mosquito netting over them. I would later learn that it served to protect one from rats as well as insects. The hut (or "hooch") was about the size of an average bedroom at home, but here, eight men lived on these cots in rather close quarters. It had a wooden floor, screen sides, without windows, and a peaked aluminum roof. Although there was electricity, only one light bulb was hanging from the ceiling. It occurred to me that this would take some getting used to. This was merely a place to sleep with a roof over my head.

Captain Anderson suggested that we go over to the Legal Office so that I could meet the other men. He pointed to a half-moon metal roof Quonset hut about 100 yards across the hillside. That was the Division Legal Office. As we walked, the captain pointed out different landmarks to me. Higher up the hill on the left was the bunker belonging to the Commanding General of the 3d Marine Division. It was set right into the hillside and built of stone and concrete. It looked very secure. On a lower level was the Mess Hall. Still further down was the Shower House. I was informed that showers were from 1700 to 1900 hours each day (5-7 PM). There was an immersion heater to warm the shower water. Most of the time it didn't work.

As we entered the legal hut, I saw three field desks with enlisted men busy typing. There were a few filing cabinets. I was introduced to the men. The typewriters looked rusty, and the documents looked damp. The men appeared not to notice. We then moved through a partition into the inner section where the lawyers and the major were located. Here, there were a few bookshelves with a smattering of weather-beaten books. Once again, I was introduced. The atmosphere did not seem overly friendly. The last section had a closed office where the colonel worked. The major and colonel would be my immediate superiors.

Captain Anderson knocked on the colonel's door with the 'salt' of a short timer, and we were told to enter. We walked in without saluting. In the Marine Corps, one doesn't wear his cover (hat) inside buildings, and one doesn't salute without the cover on. I felt like a kid on the first day of school.

"Colonel Duffy, Captain Zonderman, our new replacement is here," Anderson said. The colonel stood up and leaned over his cluttered desk to shake my hand. "Glad to have you aboard." He seemed like a friendly sort of fellow. He then sat back down, motioning me to take a seat. "Are you all set? I hope Captain Anderson got you a place to stay." "Yes, Sir," I answered. The colonel smiled. "It's not much, but it's home. Don't despair, Zonderman, you'll get used to it." The Colonel looked at Anderson and said, "And don't let any of these old soldiers scare you with their war stories." I started to relax.

The old man was a pro. He knew how to put his men at ease.

> I'm sure you will get used to the routine here. It's pretty casual. The one thing I want to be clearly understood. The workday here starts promptly at 0730. Also, you don't go anywhere out of the immediate area without checking out with us first. Well, that's about it. We'll get you all

settled tomorrow. For now, look around and familiarize yourself with the area.

I thanked the colonel. It seemed like the time to get up and leave. I felt that I had been dismissed even though I really hadn't been told anything, but things would probably start to fall into place quickly as soon as I got started. I returned the pistol, flak jacket, and helmet.

After meeting the colonel, I went back to the hut to get my gear squared away. It would be time for chow soon and I didn't want to miss that. When I arrived at the hut, some of the other officers had returned. They all looked up as I entered. For a second, I felt self-conscious. One of them moved toward me and extended his hand. "I'm Ed Drucker. Welcome to the Ritz." I smiled. "I'm Paul Zonderman." Drucker turned to the rest of the men and introduced me. They seemed like a nice bunch of guys. I sensed a sort of twinkle in their eyes as if they were holding something back. Perhaps it was to say, "you poor bastard." For them, it was good to see a new man. It made them feel closer to the time when they would be going home. Somehow, each new man that joined the end of the line made it seem to the others that they were pushed closer to the front.

They all looked worn and weary. It was wet, damp, cold and chilly. They moved slowly. If not for their toughness, one might feel that they were lost souls, just trying to do their job under very compromising conditions. The whole picture was a depressing one. The continuous rain didn't help.

I wanted to find answers for my many questions. I decided to attach myself to Drucker until I got to know the rest. Drucker seemed to be a little more communicative. He answered all my questions patiently. I didn't want to be a bother, but there was just so much that I needed to know. Among other details, Drucker mentioned that they had mortar attacks periodically, but there was nothing to worry about. There was a sandbag bunker in front of their hut. It had been built above ground since the rains would fill any hole which they might dig. The last attack had been a couple of weeks before. It had been directed further down the road. Surprisingly, the attitude toward this was very casual. Drucker advised that, "If you made it to the bunker, you're OK. If you don't, well, you don't."

After chow, some of the men went back to the legal office to play bridge or write letters. I thought about writing to Ann, but I really didn't have anything to say. Nobody really told me anything yet. I would write the next evening. Hopefully, I would have some information by then.

Later that evening, I went to the Officer's Club for a beer to help me unwind. Besides, I wanted to be alone for a while so that I could sort things out. The "O" club was a hut just like the others, but with a few more lights, some decent bamboo furniture, and a well-stocked bar. I was surprised to see the two Vietnamese waitresses, serving drinks in their traditional pajama suits. The girls were friendly, even cute, and appeared to be pals with all the soldiers. One of them approached me and asked, "You want something drink, dai-wee?" I looked at her and said, "Beer." "You never come here before. I not see you" she said, and I replied, "I just arrived." "Oh, number one" she said with a smile. I would later discover that the word 'dai-wee' meant captain, and 'number one' was an expression of approval. As I sipped my beer, I slowly felt the chill in my bones fade away. It would just take some time to get used to my surroundings.

"Excuse me, do you mind if I join you?" I looked up and saw a round smiling face topped with gray hair. I gestured toward a chair and invited the man to join me. The man was dressed in fatigues but was obviously not military. "My name is Ev Myers. I'm a war correspondent," the man said. "New in country?" Everett asked with a grin. "Yes", I said. "Does it show?"

After some friendly chat, it was time to hit the sack. I walked back to my hut. The evening had quite unexpectedly turned out to be an enjoyable one. I liked Everett. The correspondent had been around; he had seen it all. As the Navy/Marine expression went, he was 'salty.' Instead of being downtown in one of the really nice

Air Force clubs drinking with his colleagues, Everett was up in our primitive surroundings and small Officers' Club. I felt that this was indicative of his personality. He seemed to be interested in the men involved in the war, the human factor. Everett's experiences with war included over two years in country. He had also been involved in Korea and World War II.

I walked slowly back to the hut as I was unfamiliar with the area, and the path was bumpy and muddy. When I arrived, the other men were sleeping. As I fumbled with my clothes in the dark, I realized how cold and damp I was. The temperature was 50 degrees. With the light drizzle, one didn't realize that he was getting wet. There was no heat to help us dry out. The screens were bare without a window. There was no real protection from the elements. If it was wet and damp outside, it would be wet and damp inside. My clothes would be placed next to the cot when I went to sleep. In the morning, they would still be damp.

There was no way to beat it, but the resourcefulness of the GI led to various attempts to overcome the conditions. Some of the men fashioned what they called hot boxes out of old crates. These were small lockers with an electric light bulb propped up on the inside. A few key items of clothing could be placed inside. Usually, it was clothing that was being saved for R&R. The dry heat from the light bulb kept the material from becoming mildewed. I decided to build one as soon as possible. Another trick I heard about was to sleep with a pair of socks on my stomach. The body heat would partially dry them out by morning.

I pulled the damp blanket over myself. Although I was very tired, it was hard to fall asleep. The background noises disturbed me. There was the constant pop of flares going off around the perimeter. Through the screens of the hut, I could see the bursts of light in the distance. Captain Anderson had pointed out one area, called Marble Mountain, in which there was constant activity. There was a great deal of infiltration in that area, so the constant illumination was required. I knew that I would get used to the sights and sounds in time, however, it was somewhat comforting to be at such a large base. The area housed many different services (Army, Navy, Air Force and Marines), and the outer perimeter was a safe distance away. However, every time I heard a new sound, I could just picture a herd of screaming Vietnamese attacking us. Years later, I still dreamed about this. It was particularly unnerving because I had no weapon yet. The night sounds were myriad and included at least one familiar one, the screech of our low flying jets. The thump of our artillery in the distance was somewhat comforting, but still distracting.

The next morning, I felt someone shaking me. It seemed as though I had just fallen asleep. I sat up and pulled my pants and boots on over the underclothes I had slept in. Throwing my poncho over my shoulders, I ventured out in search of the latrine. I lit a cigarette while I was waiting my turn for the two-holer. After I had paid my respects to mother nature, I went down to the shower stall to shave and brush my teeth. Then I walked down to the Mess Hall with my bunk mates.

I disliked the poncho. The rubber made one sweat profusely, especially when the weather was humid. You had to decide whether to be wet from the rain or from your own sweat. When we entered the Mess Hall, we walked to the back where pegs were located. There they hung their ponchos and pistol belts. It was like a saloon from a cowboy movie. Breakfast was surprisingly decent: eggs, bread, bacon, and coffee.

After the meal, I sloshed over to the Legal Office. As I entered, I noticed that Captain Anderson was sitting down by the colonel's desk. I joined them. The colonel spoke.

> You two have already met. Captain Anderson will be rotating shortly. He is the Foreign Claims Officer for the Division. You will be taking his place. I am not going to assign you anything in particular right now. I want you to follow him around and see what he does. Particularly, I want you to go out with him when he pays the claims.

I did not respond. I hoped that my face had not shown my reaction. This was one job I did not want. The colonel turned to Captain Anderson.

> Gus, I want you to explain to Captain Zonderman here as much of the background and procedure as you can. Transfer the records to him and show him how you keep them. Also introduce him to all the people that he will have contact with. In addition to that, we've got court martials going on here all the time. You're certainly going to have duties in that regard. You will be sharing our load as trial and defense counsel. There are other jobs we are called upon to do. You will be familiarized with them as they arise, but for now, we'll start on the foreign claims. As the court martials convene, we will let you sit in on some of the more interesting ones so you can see what the procedure is here. I pretty much want you to concentrate on getting acclimated for the present. Don't worry so much about the first few days; just get yourself settled in. You'd better start by going down to supply and getting the gear that you will need.

The colonel paused for a second, evaluating me. "Well, that's all for now, captain. I'm sure that you'll fit right in here." "Thank you, Sir."

When we left the office, Captain Anderson had one of the corporals drive me to the Supply Hut about a quarter of a mile down the road. I asked the Supply Sergeant to give me everything that was needed. In addition to the regular equipment such as a helmet, flak jacket, and other gear, I needed mosquito netting for my bunk. Sometimes the insects posed as great a threat as the human enemy. After a load of equipment had been piled up, the sergeant in charge gave me some forms to fill in and sign.

Where is my .45, I asked with some amazement.

I'm sorry, Sir, you'll have to come back on that. I don't have any left.

You've got to be kidding me, I replied. What do you mean you don't have anymore?

No Sir, we're all out right now.

I stood there saying nothing. There really was nothing to say. The situation was absurd. Although I was in a base camp, it seemed very strange not to be issued a weapon. It was frightening. This was a war zone. We were drawing combat pay. How did they have the gall to tell me that they could not supply me with a weapon to defend myself? I had heard much criticism about logistical problems in Vietnam, but this was ridiculous. This was the first in a long line of 'bitches' which accounted for the bitterness of so many

of the men. It was not until a week later that I was able to procure an old .45 with holster, clip, and ammunition.

In the first week of living and working with my new colleagues, I realized that they were not wearing the same uniform. There was a strange caste system among the troops in Vietnam which became readily apparent to me after a relatively short period. At the bottom of the class structure was the newcomer. At the top of the class structure was the short timer, who had scrounged whatever he needed. Pride was based upon the fact that they had made it that far. They had seen it all. Most important, they knew all the angles. And the angles were very important. When you lived under difficult conditions, everyone would work to better his own lot. That type of living condition fostered a situation where each man tried to scratch for those few basic comforts.

One of the earliest indicia of one's position in the pecking order is the uniform. At this point, I still had my stateside utilities and leather boots. The old timers had jungle utilities and jungle boots. Jungle utilities looked a little lighter and stronger. They had big bulging pockets on the sides and chest. They were more comfortable and practical, but they were also a sign that you were 'salty.' I wanted to obtain a few pairs. My first set came through a tip. One of the men told me that someone had shipped out the day before. He might well have thrown some out. I went out to the trash can and rummaged through it. My efforts were rewarded with one pair of utilities. I promptly sent my new prize out to the Vietnamese laundry shack.

During the rainy season, Vietnamese laundries had no facilities to dry the clothes since this could not be done outdoors. Therefore, they dried the clothing over fires. It resulted in a lingering odor. I found myself smelling like a hickory smoked Marine. This was my first touch of 'salt.' I looked and smelled the part. Rummaging through the ashcan hurt my pride a little, but there was no way that these fatigues could be secured through Supply. After the problem with my weapon, this was not that surprising.

I had a similar experience when I tried to obtain a pair of jungle boots. The regular leather boots would mildew and rot in the dampness. Once they became wet, they would stay damp. One's feet were always cold. It was unpleasant to wake up in the morning and put on damp boots. There was no way to fight it.

Jungle boots were a predominantly green canvas, and a minimum of leather. They dried out more easily. They also had a little hole in the bottom so that if the water came in, it would have a way out. In addition, they had a steel plate in the sole so that a punji stake or traps would not penetrate one's foot. These could not be found in Supply or the trash, yet I looked around and everyone seemed to have a pair. After a few weeks, I got friendly with the enlisted men in the office. Finally, I decided to ask one where he had managed to come by his boots. The 'salty' corporal looked at me with a sheepish grin.

> Gee, Sir, I think that I may be able to get you a pair. Let me check. JoJo, the Vietnamese who runs the little store down in the 3rd Shore Party Battalion area, has been able to service us in the past. What size do you take?

I gave him my size and let it ride for a few days. When I checked back, I was informed that "It will take a few more days, but it will cost you." "How much," I asked. "Three cartons of cigarettes, Sir." I hadn't expected it to be free. Vietnamese certainly weren't known for doing us any favors. "I'll go out and get the cigarettes," I responded. The corporal looked up and smiled. "Make them Salem, Sir. They are fascinated by our menthol cigarettes."

I smiled. I was catching on. Very soon I had a beautiful set of jungle boots in my correct size. Coincidentally I happened to be down in Supply a few days later. I decided to inquire into the possibility of being issued some jungle boots. "Oh God no, captain. That's one of those quantities that we can't get." I was learning.

FIVE

LEARNING THE ROPES

One morning as I came into the Legal Office, I found Gus Anderson placing some papers in a tattered old briefcase which looked as if it had seen quite a few campaigns. Anderson looked up as I entered.

> Come on, old buddy. We've got to pay a few claims today. Give you a little experience outside the gate. There is nothing to worry about, Paul. We're only going to a village on the outskirts of the base. There are a half a dozen claims to be paid.
>
> How will we find all the claimants?
>
> It's easy. They'll be waiting for us at the local District Headquarters. I went down there a couple of weeks ago with a list. Then the local Chief rounds them up and tells them when we want them to be there.

Anderson opened the briefcase and checked through his papers. I noticed piles of 'piastres' (Vietnamese currency). I asked, "What's the procedure in obtaining the funds?"

> I picked up the money in dispersing yesterday while you were sitting in on that court martial. When the vouchers come in, you take them down there and sign for the money. This is the one thing that you better remember. You are on the hook for that money until you get the signature of the claimant on the receipt. You don't want

to lose it. I locked it up in the office last night. Oh, that reminds me, I have got to give you the combination. Once you have it, it's a good idea to separate the piasters into piles, one for each claim. I usually attach the corresponding papers to the money with a rubber band. It saves time later and believe me, you want to spend as little time out there as possible.

As we bounced down the muddy road, I watched the locals prodding water buffaloes with little sticks. Some waved, some ignored us. Some smiled. There was a conspicuous absence of draft age young men. Finally, they pulled into a large dirt courtyard in front of a gray stucco building, French design. There were a few Vietnamese army trucks parked to one side, and several people, including some Vietnamese soldiers, milling about.

As we left the Jeep, a few of the people nodded to Anderson. He returned their greetings. With his bushy mustache he was easily recognizable. I noticed a figure weaving his way through the crowd. The man worked his way up to Anderson and bowed. Anderson bowed and then shook hands. The man turned and they fol-

lowed. No words of English had been spoken. Apparently, this man was their liaison, and he had done this before. They were ushered through the masses to a corner of the room where Anderson could sit down at an old table. I stood next to him, my back toward the rear wall. Again, not a word was said. The procedure was routine.

I heard some leaves crackling behind me. I suddenly realized that I had my back to a large open window. I sidestepped quickly away from the window. It was merely one of the local officials outside relieving himself behind the building. I eyed the window again. It made me feel very vulnerable. I was still new in country and inclined to be looking over my shoulder. It was not really paranoia. It was just that we were out here by ourselves, surrounded by Vietnamese. It was not that I felt threatened by anything in particular. On the contrary, the people seemed very friendly. It was simply the constant exposure. Who could tell which of these villagers turned hostile at night? The one comforting thought was that we are the men bringing the piasters. If the VC started shooting up the Foreign Claims Officers, they would be cutting off the hand that was feeding them. Perhaps that was one of the reasons for Anderson's bushy mustache. He wanted everyone to recognize him as the man who brought the "P's."

Anderson had gotten his papers in order. The time had come to pay the first claim. He nodded to their liaison, who was supervising the procedure, and handed him one of the sheets. The man called out the name. Momentarily, an old woman with a wrinkled face shuffled shyly up to the table. She spoke with the local official and handed him her ID card. He in turn handed it to Anderson. The picture bore only a slight resemblance to the woman, but as Anderson indicated to me, God only knows how they take these pictures. You are safe if it bears even the slightest resemblance. Then he checked the name and copied down the ID card number. Anderson looked up at me and said, "This is one of a series of claims growing out of an air crash six months ago. One of our large transports failed on takeoff and careened into this village, which is just on the other side of the runway. Her son was one of the victims. Christ, it was a Foreign Claims Officer's nightmare. Anderson counted out the money. As he handed it to the woman, he was serious and said that he was sorry in Vietnamese. She looked at the money and signed the receipt with a thumbprint.

The rest of the claims were handled in the same manner. The only problem was with the last man. The claimants never knew how much money they would be receiving. The claim was made and then evaluated through channels. This man did not feel the award was sufficient. Captain Anderson told the translator to explain to the man that he would return the case to the claims people and inform them that it had been refused. However, he advised that although they would review the claim, there was no guarantee that a greater amount would be forthcoming. In any event, it would take some time before any further disposition would be made. The man still decided that this was not enough. "He say he want more." Anderson acquiesced, replacing the money in the folder in his briefcase. Maybe the man would get more and maybe not. It was of no concern to Gus. When this was completed, he got up, bowed, and left. Once we had finished, the job seemed less ominous to me. However, I just wanted to get back to the relative safety of the camp as soon as possible.

After a few weeks in country, I was just beginning to feel at home in Danang. It was then that the colonel called me into his office and informed me that they were setting up a 3rd Division forward up North in Phu Bai. Ultimately, the headquarters of the 3rd Marine Division would be relocated there. The 1st Marine Division would be moving up to Danang from Chu Lai to take their place. Because of the many incidents in the forward area, the higher brass wanted a Foreign Claims Officer stationed there immediately. Captain Anderson, a sergeant, and I would be leaving as soon as possible. The colonel felt that since Anderson would normally be there alone, it would be a good opportunity for me to learn the ropes and take over at Phu Bai where we would be heading.

I decided to write a letter to Ann before I moved North to Phu Bai. When I wrote my letters, I felt close to her for those moments. Anything which anyone had ever said about writing to a serviceman overseas was absolutely true. The value of a letter from home cannot be overstated. The familiar words of a loved one are comforting. They served to reassure me that another world was waiting for me, something warm, loving, and safe. It was also very exciting to receive the occasional package. When I had asked Ann to send me a pair of rubber mud boots, she had to send them one at a time to accommodate the weight allowance for packages. It was a month between receiving boot number one and boot number two. When everything seemed dim, such as now with my new orders, communicating with Ann would raise my spirits.

After I had been in country for a short time, I bought a small Japanese battery powered tape recorder at the PX in Danang. Once a week I would record a half hour tape and send it home. Ann would share the tape with my parents, then record over it with news from home, and send it back to me. It was always thrilling when I walked into my office and saw that a letter or tape had come for me. When everyone had gone back to the Officers Club or the office at night, I would lie back on my bunk and play the tape in the privacy of my hut. Then I would take her tape from the week before, and record over it. A major problem for me was how much to tell her. I was direct. If we had a mortar attack, she might read about it elsewhere and imagine the worst. Often, I would spice it up with humor. I soft-pedalled the Foreign Claims missions as much as possible. The letters or tapes to and from servicemen were sent free of charge.

Anderson and I would go North by air, and the sergeant would follow by convoy with the office equipment. Phu Bai and Hue (pronounced as Way) were in the same neighborhood off Route 1. The city of Hue was the ancient capital and was fairly built-up. From Phu Bai, the Marines also occupied North to Dong Ha, which was adjacent to the Demilitarized Zone (DMZ). That was like the 38th parallel in Korea.

SIX

WELCOME TO PHU BAI

After chow the following morning, Gus and I had one of the enlisted men drive us down to the airfield. The Jeep pulled up in front of a big aluminum hanger which served as a terminal. Inside there were several cages. We joined the line in front of the window for Phu Bai. When my turn came, I handed a copy of my travel orders to the young clerk. I was handed a tag with #41 printed on it. Stepping away, one had to watch where one walked since the floor was a mass of bodies, most of the men asleep, with their steel helmets serving as pillows. We sat down in an empty spot on the floor next to the wall. There were no scheduled flights. We would wait until there was room on a plane heading up to Phu Bai. Sensing my travel companion was in his usual non talkative mood, I tried to get a little sleep. At least it would make the time go faster. If the rain got really bad, the non-crucial flights might be grounded. There was no telling how long it would take.

Then I was awakened by the loudspeaker. "Numbers 31 through 60, report to the C-130 on the line." Anderson nudged me. "They are playing our tune," he said. We picked up our gear and worked our way through the human maze to the door. We sloshed through mud, then onto the asphalt runway, and headed to the doorway of the plane. A sergeant checked our number tags and we boarded. I sat on the floor next to a big crate. The plane was mud spattered, wet, and crowded as usual, but I was not overly concerned about where I sat. The flight was short, taking less than a half hour.

As soon as we disembarked in Phu Bai, I knew that this was a different ballpark than the one I had been playing in. The only similarity would be the stakes were the same. This was not the sprawling organized city complex that Danang had been. Phu Bai was only a Marine Corps forward position. It was flat, muddy country. The airstrip here was much smaller than the one in Danang, and not able to accommodate jets.

We headed for a large structure which served as a terminal. After looking around a bit, we concluded we would have to bum a ride to the Headquarters area about a half mile away. We walked in heavy rain to the muddy dirt road. We waited until a jeep came by which bore the insignia of the 3rd Marine Division.

Anderson asked the driver to let us off near the Informational Services Office (ISO). Colonel Duffy had told him that there were no shacks set up at Phu Bai for the Division Legal. We would set up office in the corner of the ISO shack. These are the men in charge of putting out press releases.

When we arrived at the headquarters area, we thanked the driver and walked into the ISO shack. The major, who was in charge, wasn't overly friendly. The ISO people weren't overjoyed about giving up a quarter of their already overcrowded shack. Those were the orders, and we would set up shop here when the convoy came up from Danang with our equipment.

The ISO major directed us to the hut where we would be living. As we walked over, I looked around. The area was under construction. There was a great deal of building which still had to be done before it would be the new headquarters for the 3rd Marine Division. At that point in time, it would be the home for a two-star general. Some of the units stationed there were still living in tents. The area in which Gus and I would be located was built up a bit more.

We walked into one of the huts. It had a wooden floor raised a few feet off the ground. All the sides had screening mounted on a wooden skeleton. There were rolls of drab olive canvas which could be rolled down over the sides to keep out the wind and rain. It was much the same as my first home in Danang, one light bulb and no running water.

I selected an empty cot and threw my gear down on the floor next to it. Flopping down on the bunk, I lit a cigarette. I was careful not to get the mud from my boots on the paper-thin mattress. This was the life, and there was at least one plus. We would be our own bosses. There would be nobody from Legal to answer to as long as we met our responsibilities. For the remainder of the day, we got ourselves settled. All my worldly goods were in my footlocker next to my bed.

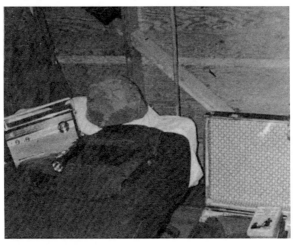

I decided to walk around the area and get acclimated. I went alone since Anderson preferred to sleep. The major facilities such as Communications and the Tactical Operations Center were built underground. They were protected by layers of sandbags, and radio antennas dotted the upper surface. In the center of the headquarters area was a row of huts which served as the offices for the various staff sections. Division Legal would be located here. The Mess Hall, Disbursing Office, Post Office, and PX were bigger and better constructed. This was not a base, but a forward position. The area looked isolated and vulnerable. It was closer to the DMZ, and I sensed it.

Back at my new home that evening, I pulled off my soggy clothes and put my sweatsuit on over my underwear. It was cold and raw. I slid under my blanket, adjusting the mosquito netting over the bed. As I lay there, I heard artillery firing constantly. It was louder and more frequent than at Danang. I had been told that this was 'H&I' firing (Harassment and Interdiction). The 155 Howitzers were very loud if the muzzle was aimed in your direction. The sound produced a startling reaction which caused me to rise a foot horizontally off my bunk. Yet, this was one of our best defenses. We randomly peppered outside the Marine perimeter to prevent Viet Cong infiltration into the camp area.

I had been told that it would probably take me weeks before I could begin to get a good night's sleep. Finally, I did get to sleep. My mind began the slow process of filtering out the outgoing sounds from the incoming sounds.

The next thing I was aware of was the sound of doors slamming in the distance. Bang, bang, bang. The door slamming sound got nearer and louder. I heard voices. I lay there half awake. I heard the door of the hut next to us slam. Then, someone opened our door and yelled "incoming." In a second, I went from almost sleeping to 150% awareness. As I had imagined so many times before, I rolled out of my cot sideways into a low crouch and donned my flak jacket and steel helmet. Then I scrambled for the door staying as low as possible to present less of a target for the deadly spray of shrapnel. I dove out the screen door, bumping into others, all heading for the four-foot-high sandbag bunker on the side of the hut. I rolled over the top, doing a bellyflop into the mud puddle inside. To my surprise, I was one of the first into the bunker. A second later, I felt a body land squarely upon me, pushing me even deeper into the mud. I didn't mind. It was that much more protection. We just lay there shivering in the cold as the incoming explosion noises drew closer. To my amazement, I found myself praying. "God, let me live through this night." I felt helpless. There was nothing to do but wait. Death was being showered upon us in a random fashion. Would we take a direct hit? They say that you never hear the one that gets you. It was over a few minutes later. As we started climbing out of the bunker, I heard voices nearby calling for a medic as well as nearby moans. It had been quite bad for some. Someone nearby said, "I wonder which friendly village that came from." This was a reference to the fact that the Viet Cong often parked their mortars on the edge of a friendly village so that the base would not return fire. I went back into my hut, sat on my bed, and touched the "Chai" medal my mother had given me, now attached to my dog tags.

The next few months passed quickly. All the Marines kept little charts with a box for each day or week remaining in their tour of duty. Anderson's artwork had almost all the remaining squares filled in. He had been like most short timers. He tried to find a hole for himself. He had wound up his responsibilities. He had no new projects to begin. All he had to do was stay alive for a few more days. He was extremely withdrawn and tightlipped. I had learned a great deal from Gus Anderson. He knew his job. Soon, he rotated out, and I was the Foreign Claims Officer of the 3rd Marine Division.

I was kept busy by "Jag Manual Investigations." In this bureaucratic system, it was common to convene an investigation whenever government property was lost or destroyed. Any commanding officer could convene one of these investigations. Somebody was always responsible. There was also the documentation of atrocities. I recall being called to the makeshift infirmary in Phu Bai to document the injuries of an American officer who had been taken prisoner by the North Vietnamese. He had been tied to a tree, sliced up, and left to die. When I saw him at the field infirmary, laying in a bed, all I saw was the top half of his body totally wrapped in bandages including his head. He could barely speak. I wasn't going to question him. There was nothing more I could report. The conflict between the North and South was vicious. It was their civil war.

I also recall being enroute somewhere in a helicopter. Looking down as I viewed the countryside, I saw scattered strange white X's in the treetops. I asked the Marine sitting next to me, what that was. He explained that the South Vietnamese interrogated three prisoners at a time up in our U.S helicopters. If number one refused to talk, he was thrown out of the copter. So too with number two. By the time they reached number three, the man was willing to 'spill the beans.' Those white X's were spread-eagled dead bodies. The images will never be erased from my mind.

On the more civilized side, I occasionally set up legal assistance sessions. Guys would grab flights or bum rides in. I travelled to the outlying units when necessary. One of my most common chores was drafting Wills. Although the men were encouraged to handle this stateside before they left, many did not have one. They were young and didn't worry about such things. I would ask them some questions and then have a will typed up which suited their needs.

Another common problem involved unpaid bills at home. Often, Marines would receive dunning letters threatening to sue them. I would point out the 'Soldiers and Sailors Civil Relief Act' and tell them not to sweat it. No one could sue them until they returned home. In rare instances, I might recommend Emergency Leave, but I would have to be prepared to answer to higher authority to accomplish that. The 'Dear John' letter was the most frustrating. It was all too common. I would often refer these matters to a Chaplain down in Danang.

There was a tendency among young Marines to play "quick-draw" like they played as kids. If a round was accidentally left in their pistol, some innocent soldier nearby would be dead. The maximum penalty was seldom levied. It was usually 'Negligent Homicide', and the more culpable cases resulted in 'Involuntary Manslaughter' prosecution. It was rather difficult to get these men off entirely unless I could get an armorer to examine the weapon and testify that it discharged because of faulty mechanisms. This was rare. No one is supposed to have a round in the chamber while in a base camp.

SEVEN

ROUTINE DUTIES

At Phu Bai, all the officers had to take their share of combat-related jobs, regardless of their primary classification. My day to be the Perimeter Watch Officer had come. The heart of the Phu Bai base was surrounded by an outer circumference or perimeter of barbed wire. There was an inner circumference of two-man foxholes spaced about twenty feet apart. Each position was occupied at sunset by two Marines. They had telephone lines to talk to the Perimeter Watch Officer who was in an underground bunker, covered by planks and canvas, and equipped with radios, maps, and a lantern.

In the afternoon, before the troops arrived, I would go to my bunker site within the perimeter and then go out and inspect the positions on the perimeter. On this day, I was in a Jeep with a driver slowly moving around the circumference. I checked to see if the Claymore mines were properly placed. It was a good thing that I did this because I found one Claymore facing inward. I carefully turned it to face outward.

Soon, truckloads of Marines arrived, dismounted, and formed for instruction in the bleachers. I thought to myself that here I was, a lawyer, commanding this band of men defending the outer limits of the Phu Bai base. This was why all Marine officers were given infantry training. I addressed the men.

> I'll make this brief. I want absolute fire discipline. I don't want anybody taking pot shots at anything unless you get clearance from me over the land line. I don't want twenty

guys giving away their positions just because you think you hear something. Our barbed wire has empty beer cans with rocks in them attached to the wire as noisemakers. The VC often drive a buffalo into the wire to make noise and draw your fire. Don't be misled. If you think you hear anything, call me. I'll get some mortar illumination. You save those grenades and automatic weapons unless you are under real attack. In that case, you don't have to wait for permission to fire.

The men would then be driven around to their holes, and I went to my underground bunker. It was hot and humid, and the mosquitos were oppressive. I studied the large map attached on the dirt wall above my makeshift desk. It showed the perimeter, the numbered foxholes, and locations of pre-planned artillery concentration spots. Soon, I took off my helmet and flak jacket so I wouldn't sweat as much in the dark silence. The waiting was endless and tense. Somewhere in the night, the internal phone buzzed. A Marine reported he heard noises to his front at hole 42. I looked at the map and saw that the closest target was concentration 236. I cranked the telephone. "Mortar platoon, Gunnery Sergeant Cleary speaking, Sir." "This is Captain Zonderman. Give me three rounds of illumination on spot 236." Within seconds, I heard the three thumps of our mortar rounds being fired in the distance. Then I heard the 'pops' as the flares ignited and slowly drifted down, lighting the area involved. Nothing was reported visible. Fortunately, this was a false alarm. The rest of the night was quiet. In the morning, the

trucks came for the men, and I headed back to the Legal Office after catching breakfast in the Mess Hall.

Later that day, I was at my desk going over some claims paperwork when there was a knock at the door. I was told that there was a village woman at the Provost Marshall's Office who wants to make a claim. I told the PMO messenger to bring her up, but make sure you have your interpreter with you.

The corporal returned with a small Vietnamese woman dressed in the traditional black pajamas and large straw hat. As she entered, she bowed low, and I returned the bow saying, "Chow Ba" (hello, mam). She took a seat, and I asked the interpreter to get her story.

The interpreter related that her little boy was run over by a U.S. truck, his legs were hurt, and they took him away. I asked further background questions knowing the details needed in the claim form I would fill out. I learned that the accident happened the day before, a couple of miles down the road near the dump. She said that it was a five-truck convoy and one of them had a green triangle on the door. The boy, Ngo, was playing beside the road and the truck hit him. She asked for one hundred thousand (100,000) piasters. She said she could not write, so I gave her an ink pad for a thumbprint. I told her I would inquire about the boy's condition, which she had not asked about. Her boy's condition seemed to be secondary to her claim. We went through a bowing routine, and the lady was taken back to the gate.

As there was nothing else pressing, I decided to start my investigation. After I put on my helmet and flak jacket, I left the office and went to the Division Motor Transport office. The real clue was that it happened near the dump. Garbage had a certain value over here: they supposedly used it to feed their animals. I was of the opinion some boys had jumped on the moving truck to steal garbage, and Ngo had fallen off the truck. I figured that these kids were no different than the street urchins of World War II who stole everything they could get their hands on.

I entered the motor pool office, introduced myself to Sergeant Sid Munter, and asked him to check his records to see if he had a small convoy on Route 9 about three miles down the road yesterday at about 1500 hours. The sergeant checked his records and said that they didn't have any trucks in that area at that time. I asked which unit had the green triangle on the door. The Sergeant identified it as being the 9th Motor T Battalion. I thanked him and went back to my office. I looked it up in my directory and then picked up the field phone saying, "Shove, Give me Penguin," and then, "Penguin, give me 426." Sergeant Carter answered the phone, and I told him what I was investigating. The sergeant recognized the incident.

> Oh, yeah, that little dink who jumped on one of our trucks trying to steal garbage. Sir, we ought to post guards. Those little bastards drive us nuts.

As I hung up the field phone, I plotted my course of action. This wasn't a combat-related injury. It couldn't be related to a tactical maneuver. This was a non-combat claim, in which cases I had jurisdiction and the military would pay the claim. I handwrote a letter for Corporal Parker to type later. It would be from the Commanding General to the Battalion Commander involved requesting a Jag-Manual investigation into the injuries sustained by Ngo Luc on the day in question.

In the interim, I found out that the boy had been treated at a local aid station, and then medevac'd to a field hospital in Danang. The boy would be all right except for a slight limp, which would keep him out of the draft.

It was a month later before the jungle of red tape had been penetrated and the pay voucher came back. I went down to the Disbursing Officer, and returned to my office with the cash, which I put in the safe.

Usually, I would wait until I had a few claims to pay before I went out. This was an exception. The next day, I procured a Jeep, an armed driver, and an armed escort. We left the safety of the camp armed with their M-14 rifles and drove down Route 1 toward the village. I had made the exception because the old lady lived close to the base, and I felt sorry for this mother who didn't know what happened to her boy. It also brought me face to face with all the misery in this primitive country. In my mind it was not my problem, but my emotions did not agree with my intellect.

Rising somewhat from my seat from the impact of a bump, which seemed to be the grand finale of a rocky trip, we pulled up in front of the village headquarters. It was a white stucco building abandoned by the French some years before. As we got out of the Jeep, a Marine sergeant approached us and saluted. I explained my mission and asked if they had an interpreter who could accompany me. The sergeant complied and left to get the Village Chief and an interpreter.

The Sergeant was part of a "CAC" unit of about twelve Marines living in the village, whose mission was to protect the village Chief from Viet Cong reprisals for remaining loyal to Saigon. The VC knew exactly where they were, and they had no real protection other than the radio contact with the nearby base.

The sergeant returned with a Lance Corporal Brock and an old Vietnamese civilian, Wang Ho, the Village Elder. The corporal told

us that Madame Luc lived over the rise about a half mile. He also told them that they have had some Viet Cong activity in the last few days, and that he would try to get some Vietnamese soldiers (ARVN – Army of the Republic of Vietnam) to accompany us.

After several minutes, two truckloads of ARVN joined us, and we headed back down the road. The ARVN's got out first and made a circle around the claimant's grass shack, facing outward. Their interpreter moved forward. The woman appeared at the door, saw me and bowed, and asked us to enter. I told the Viet soldier acting as interpreter to tell her that I was there to pay her claim. She bowed and gestured a thank you. She sat at the table, and I checked her ID. I then handed her the receipt to sign with a thumb print. She used my ink pad and made her impression. I then handed her 100,000 piasters. I was not sure of the value of the piaster, but I guessed it was ten cents on the dollar.

I looked around the hut. There were two straw cots, a makeshift table, shelves, two chairs, and an altar with religious items on it. I wondered what she would do with the money. She would be lucky if she could keep any of it. It would depend upon who got there first, the CAC protectors or the VC. And where would she keep it? There was no bank to deposit it in. The US paid out a lot of money in claims, but nobody can guess where it ended up.

Then she asked what happened to the boy. I replied that he will be back soon, and he will have only a limp. Her tone and demeanor did not change. It appeared that this was a parenthetical issue. In this community, the mortality rate was great, and the average life expectancy was forty years. The average farmer made the equivalent of forty cents a week.

As I made ready to leave, the old woman was walking toward us with a teapot and some moldy cups. I didn't want to offend her, but local food was poison to an American. It had something to do with the bacteria. I had learned my lesson the hard way by tasting some cookies made by the local nuns. I acted like I didn't see her, and I dashed out the door.

The ARVN patrol returned to escort my Jeep out of the woods onto a decent road. I could not help thinking about the average citizen's life here. They do not appear to feel sorry for themselves. They seem to accept the inevitability of their poor lot.

EIGHT

A LETTER TO MY DAD

While preparing the materials for this book, I found a letter I wrote to my father after I was in Vietnam for about 6 weeks. It was a man to man, veteran to veteran letter. It is reproduced below, and it is not fiction. Names of men in country have been blocked out. Family and friend's names are authentic. (Text follows.)

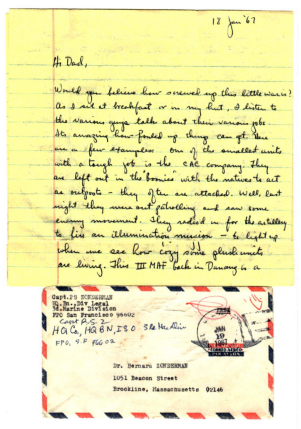

18 Jan 1967

Hi Dad,

Would you believe how screwed up this little war is? As I sit at breakfast or in my hut, I listen to the various guys talk about their various jobs. It's amazing how fouled up things can get. Here are a few examples: One of the smallest units with a tough job is the CAC Company. They are left out in the "boonies" with the natives to act as outposts – they are often attacked. Well, last night they were out patrolling and saw some enemy movement. They radioed in for the artillery to fire an illumination mission – to light up the area of a suspected enemy. It wasn't until one hour and fifteen minutes later that the first flare shot was sent up. Naturally, the enemy had passed by them. After the first round was fired, the artillery asked (on radio) if the CAC wanted a second round. A bit aggravated, CAC said, no thanks, they'd just wait for the daylight to come. Why does this happen? Before they will fire the illumination, they must inspect the map to make sure the empty illumination shells won't fall on a house of the natives. This is such a polite little war. The CAC unit could have been wiped out. How about this - - when CAC calls in to request for artillery, they have to give the compass bearing between themselves and the target. This is fine, but CAC has no compasses. They rate them, but there are none in supply to give them.

The troops out on operation Chinook are in miserable condition. They all have bad colds or pneumonia, and most of their feet are pussy and festered with "immersion foot" (from living in the water). The C.O. of 3/26 (on Operation Chinook) was just relieved because of the many accidents in that unit. One kid dropped a grenade in a tent and blew up 10 of his buddies. Kids are accidentally shooting each other, and some are doing it on purpose just to get away. One of my bunkmates, XXX, Army, is with "Chinook" and he can't believe the miserable equipment the Marines have. In his opinion, the higher ups just don't take care of the subordinates. Marines are supposed to get along with nothing, and that's what they have. Since XXX is in the Army, he has a tent as good as the Colonel's (C.O.) tent. At least the Army seems to equip its people and look out for their health and comfort.

It's amazing how fouled up things get by the time you get down to the unit level. You can just laugh when the politicians say that our troops are getting every kind of support. I think we spend more money on helping Vietnamese than on helping our troops. Most of the rice, we give the natives – in bags with the handclasp of friendship printed on them - most of this is captured from the VC who always seem to get it.

And then, there are our allies, the Vietnamese. Here's an experience that XXX, and other bunkmates had -- There was a truck of supplies to be unloaded at a Viet military camp. A platoon of Viets was standing around and a Viet Captain ordered them to unload. They ignored him. They would only take orders from their 2nd lieutenant platoon leader. Christ, how can you do anything with help like that? I guess the newspapers don't talk about the lack of pride or cowardliness or unreliability of the Vietnamese troops. Would you believe they are sensitive? Yes, they often break into tears if you get mad at them. xxx has an interpreter to whom he gave a week's leave. One month later, he came back. In Vietnam, they are not UA (unauthorized absence) until after a month.

Anybody who works closely with Vietnamese really hates them. They'd honestly like to kill them. Most often when you find a Viet Cong casualty, he has been over-killed with enthusiasm – maybe 20 bullets in him. Many guys are mad because you can't even go to the "O" club without seeing a Vietnamese waitress giggling and screaming. People end up hating the place and the people. This is added to the aggravation we have when we see how cozy some plush units are living. The III MAF back in Danang is a continual source of aggravation.

Did you know that you get a $500/month tax exemption for any month by just being here for one day in a month? So, what does the Commandant xxx do? Every two months, he makes a two-day inspection tour. He comes on the 31st of one month and leaves on the first of the next month. This way, by coming for a total of 12 days, 6 times, he gets a year of deducting $500/ month for taxes.

I'm very grateful that I am part of Headquarters Battalion and live a lot better than the troops in the field. These problems I see or hear about don't directly affect me, but it makes me mad anyway. This isn't *supposed to be a war, but to the guys who are getting shot at, wounded, maimed - it makes little difference what they call it on paper.*

So, I'll do my part and be proud I am here, but the whole thing leaves a bad taste in my mouth. As we say, "It's a bag of worms." The only consolation is that as bad as our situation seems, we're still ten times better than the opponents. Given some supplies, some real support, and a green light, we could really mop up this place. But what's the point – by the time our last man had pulled out, the VC would be in control again. It seems like this thing has no real solution, and in that respect, I sympathize with Johnson.

As for my own job in settling some of these claims, I could do them so much faster if there was a vehicle at my disposal. It seems that the motor pool has only 1 or 2 Jeeps to serve as taxis. When you are lucky enough to get one, that doesn't do any good since there is an order that you need two vehicles together before you can leave the base. This is just to drive into Hue (Way). Is Hue dangerous? Though it's off limits to Marines not on official business, the Army has a MACV (Military Assistance Command Vietnam) compound there. The other services have free access, and even have dances and parties there, and stay in the local hotel.

My Clerk-Typist got orders to another unit, so for the past several days, I've had nobody to do up the reports etc. I have to turn out. This is an example of the great efficiency. It seems like no matter what your job, each day holds some major crisis. These are almost always caused by lack of communication or delayed mail messages, or other foul-ups. If our telephone system alone was reliable, 90% of the problems could be straightened out in a few minutes. I suppose I should let it suffice by saying that the situation is very frustrating. There is nothing heroic about us here – it's just a nagging day-by-day pain in the ass.

I received the tape you sent, and I thank you. I have access to other tape machines, so I can play most any kind of tape you want to send. It was pleasant hearing all the voices from home – Ed and Alice, the Polans, etc., - even Fanny. Thanks for Amy's Bat Mitzvah part also. I am enclosing a picture of the camera I got. It cost $44 here. Had I used my head, I would have borrowed your Minox before I left. By the way, *the new Minox, with built in meter, costs about $100 here. I think I will apply for my first five-day R&R in Hong Kong about March. By then I should have enough $ saved to make the trip worthwhile. Marty has reaffirmed his desire to form a partnership when I get home. I suppose this is what I'll do if Sidney doesn't come up with some dreamy offer. So long for now.*

Love, Paul

NINE

THE GIBSON TRIAL

Shortly after Anderson had left, the whole Division Legal staff moved up to Phu Bai. They had taken over four huts. Colonel Duffy had one. His assistant Staff Legal Officer, a major, was in the second, which also housed me and my fellow trial lawyers. The third hut was for the enlisted men, the clerk typists and court reporters. The fourth was kept vacant and was used as a primitive courtroom.

I enjoyed having friends up here whom I could talk to. I had to start getting into the office on time. This was hard sometimes when I had been kept up by mortar or rocket attacks the night before. On one of these mornings, I looked up as Major Linnehan called my name. "Paul, would you come over here for a minute." I got up and walked across the hut to the desk of Major Linnehan.

> Here is a copy of an incident report out of PMO at Dong Ha. Looks like we're going to have a rape Court Martial. Some Pfc up there may have raped a Vietnamese girl. The commanding general is going to convene an Article 32 investigation. I'm assigning you to the case. If it goes through with a General Court, I'd like you to prosecute it. So, hang with it from the start. You better get up there and see that the evidence is properly presented for the Article 32. Bill Barnard will be assigned as defense counsel. Get together with Bill and go up there tomorrow and let me know what's happening. We'll cut the orders appointing some officer up there as Investigating Officer.

Yes, Sir. Do you have any further instructions for me?

Take the report. The Marine's name is David Gibson. He's with the 3rd Engineer Battalion.

I took the folder back to my desk and started to go through it. The report had originated in the Provost Marshall's office up North in Dong Ha, which was now the new Third Division forward, adjacent to the DMZ. The incident report indicated that there was an alleged rape committed by one Private Gibson. The colonel had probably been handed this one at the general's staff conference that morning, and the Article 32 investigation would be initiated. As I started to read the report, the major called me back to his desk.

By the way, Paul, I had forgotten. This is your first rape case here. You'll have a lot of problems. This won't be an easy one. Jim Burke blew the last two rape cases we had up there (Dong Ha). You get these girls all set and everything seems fine until it comes time to testify. Then they're too sensitive to talk about what happened to them. Bang. You get yourself an acquittal. It's tough. You must work through interpreters. It can be touchy. Talk to Jim about it. He can point out some of the pitfalls. Let's stay on top of this one from the beginning. We don't want to blow another one.

I returned to my desk. I now had two hats to wear. One was for the defense; the other was representing the government by prosecuting. But in a case like this, I didn't mind prosecuting if I believed the man was guilty. A case like this was bad news. We needed the support of the people in this war. If our men went around raping sixteen-year-old girls, we'd be heading for trouble. It meant many more enemies for us and that many more friends for the Viet Cong. This man's act could cause the death of comrades.

I continued to read through the file and start one of my own. I looked up a few areas in the Court Martial Manual and the Uniform Code of Military Justice (UCMJ) to refresh my memory of the law involved in rape cases. I made some notes as I went along. I would also try to get the story from the girl as soon as possible. One of the most important things would be to check with Jim to find out who was a good interpreter to work with up there.

That evening I saw Jim Burke at the Officers Club. I asked him if he had heard about my new case.

> Yes, good luck. They're a bitch. It's hard as hell to get one of those girls to come out and testify that some big Marine 'split her uprights.' It's hard enough to convey the facts in this type of situation without going through an intermediary. Christ, that's what screwed me on the last one. You know, they have a custom here, when a girl is bad, they cut off all her hair. Well, the defense council got a little dirty. He asked the girl, 'Isn't it true that if your father found out that you were hanging around Marines, he would cut off all your hair?' And she answered 'yes'. Then he went on. 'Isn't it true that was the reason why you told the MPs that you were raped? She said 'yes.' Shit, Paul, that bastard was guilty as hell. Obviously, she didn't understand the question. Who knows how the hell that went through the interpreter? It really made it look like she had made up the story. I'm damn sure she hadn't. I had talked with her, through an interpreter, a few times. I spoke with her parents - - the whole bit. After the Article 32, there was no question that a General Court should be convened. There was no way to recover it. It's so damn imprecise trying to converse that way. I felt awful about it. But she will still get her foreign claims money. There's no need for proof beyond a reasonable doubt for that purpose, but I feel bad for them. It was so damn awkward trying to get them to talk. They don't want trouble; especially after that, they don't trust

JUSTICE IN THE JUNGLE | 63

us. They were afraid of reprisals, but I told them, no, we wanted to punish this man. I felt like we let them down. Any witnesses?

I think I've got a couple.

Well just go over it with them. Make sure they know what you're going to ask them. Take a little more time in preparation than you normally do. Make sure you use the same interpreter all the way through. If they ask the question in a different way, you might get two different answers back.

Can you suggest anybody?

Let's see. Yes, I think his name was Chan. I don't know whether that's a nickname or his real name. He's really good.

I then saw Bill Barnard, my opponent, and called him over. "Hey Bill, we need to get up to Dong Ha tomorrow and poke around on this. Shall we travel up there together?" "Yeah, I guess I'll go."

As was Captain Anderson, Bill was a short timer and 'salty,' talking like it was an imposition. "Well, how do you figure we're going to get up there," I asked. "I called last night. We'll get a lift to the airstrip. I'll meet you by the shack about 8:00 o'clock. I also hear there's a convoy going up tomorrow morning. We could grab a ride up with the Motor T battalion. We'll try the air terminal first." I shrugged my shoulders. "I'll see you tomorrow morning."

I put my gear together a little different than usual for this trip. I carried a beat-up valise with my papers. It also carried a few changes of underwear and my sweatsuit to sleep in just in case we had to stay up North a few days. Although the base would be secure from ground attacks, there was always the threat of being so close to the DMZ. In addition to rocket and mortar attacks, there was the threat of direct artillery fire from over the border.

The next morning, we went to the airstrip first, and asked the clerk what our chances were of getting a flight to Dong Ha. He responded, "I don't know Sir. The one that usually goes there has been diverted over to Khe San. Doesn't look too good Sir. They are having some problems out there and need to be re- supplied."

We then walked through the mud to where the convoy was forming up and hitched a ride. Bill walked up to a young 2nd lieutenant and said, "I'm Captain Barnard. This is Captain Zonderman from Division Legal. We're going to bum a ride up to Dong Ha." "OK, sure Sir. Hop on a truck".

We split up and picked different trucks to impose upon. I always picked a garbage truck and avoided one with ammunition or strategic equipment. I wanted a truck that the enemy wouldn't be particularly interested in blowing up. I hopped in next to the driver. This would be more comfortable then riding in the rear with the garbage.

As the gears started grinding, I looked ahead. We were heading out to Route 1, the North-South highway. As we moved along, we passed by villagers walking along the road. Some of them were on bicycles, others walked along bent over by the bundles they carried. After half an hour, I was almost hypnotized by the steady clank-clank of the windshield wipers. It would be another hour before arriving at Dong Ha. My thoughts drifted back to my last tape from Ann. She sounded like she was doing well. I hoped that this was true. It was hard to be separated at a time like this. I loved her very much. If she was scared or hurt, I felt that I was, even if I never knew the specifics.

Suddenly, my thoughts were shattered. There was an explosion, loud, rumbling, and shaking. A fraction of a second later, my truck came to a sudden stop. "Christ, we are under attack." I jumped out of the truck and crouched down by the side of the road. I didn't want to go too far onto the shoulder because of mines or punji pits. Men were hopping out of their trucks all the way up the line. Five or six trucks up, I could see one on its back, completely off the road.

Smoke was billowing forth. As I moved up, I could hear groans of agony. Ahead, there was a gaping hole in the road. One of the Marines was standing by the truck. "What was it; a mine?" I asked. "Hell no, that was a bomb. Some Gook must have been watching as we came through and detonated it electronically."

I saw a couple of Corpsmen run up to attend to the wounded. The convoy Commander had turned his jeep around and came racing back down the road. As his Jeep came to a halt, I could see him talking on a handset. He was calling in a medevac chopper to take the wounded out. He was also asking for a few gunships to survey the area just in case. I stepped up to the edge of the crowd so I could be seen in case the assistance of another officer was necessary. The Commander started having men fill in the hole so we could proceed. As I got back to my truck, I could see the medevac helicopter overhead. They certainly didn't waste any time.

I knew I had to turn away and forget it, but in just a few seconds the life of one of the men had been irrevocably changed. No single thing that he did was the cause. We were all hypervigilant. At any moment, a sniper a distance away, could take that deadly shot, or detonate a bomb. This was the reality or unreality of war.

After more delay, the convoy moved slowly on. It was a long and tiring trip, with overhanging clouds and rain. Finally, the convoy pulled off Route 1 and onto a smaller road. Then we grinded to a halt in a flat, open expanse, on an area where a base camp had been set up. I got out and slogged through the mud to what appeared to be a headquarters area. I checked in with the Commanding Officer (CO), telling him that I would be spending a few days there. The CO called over a sergeant and directed him to find me a cot in the Transient Hut next to Supply. At Dong Ha, our temporary housing was a bit primitive, although the sandbags were comforting.

I bumped into Bill Barnard as we left the CO's hut. Now that we were both up there, we wouldn't be working with each other. We were opponents, friendly enemies.

I had kept my driver and asked him to take me to the PMO's office (Provost Marshal). I walked in and asked for the lieutenant. "Can I help you" a voice asked from the other side of the room. "I'm the OIC (Officer in Charge), Lieutenant Wilkey. I've been expecting you. This is a bad scene. The villagers are up in arms about it." "Tell me about it."

> It happened in the dump area. A lot of Vietnamese hang around there. They stay just outside the wire. We tell them time and time again to stay the hell out of there, but they're like scavengers. Apparently, Gibson and two other men were on detail up there. It was their job to keep an eye on things. I'm not that clear on exactly what they were supposed to be doing.
>
> Well, this girl, she's about 16, was up there with a few older women from the village. The old ladies watched it all from a safe distance. We have statements from them.

I'd like to see them.

Fine Sir. We can take a ride down to their village.

Good. That brings up another problem. I'll need a good interpreter. One of our staff recommend a guy by the name of Chan. Do you know him?

Oh, yeah. Chan's good. Located with the headquarters. If he's around, we can grab him.

Outstanding. Go on with the story.

Well, that's just about all we've got. Afterwards, one of the old women went back to help her. The girl staggered back into the dump area, crying. They went up to a little shack on the edge where they have a sergeant in charge. He called us. He took her down to the medical station. While she was there, we brought down an interpreter and got her story. And of course, it was communicated to me. I immediately started an investigation. I checked on the roster and found out who had dump duty that day. It was three men from Alpha Company, Third Engineers. I brought them down to PMO and had the girl view them in a line-up.

Tell me about the lineup.

Well, it was a normal procedure. We had four black men, including Gibson, and the other two men from the dump, all of similar appearance. At that time, she identified Gibson. That was it, as far as I went. We wrote him up on charges and then it was sent to your office for prosecution.

OK. An Article 32 has been convened. We'll have it this Thursday. I'll have to prepare the evidence to wrap this up. I'm going to need the girl, the women, and the medical testimony.

I'll put you on also to describe the identification. That should be sufficient. First, I want to speak to the girl.

Okay. We can go down in my Jeep.

They bumped along the road until they came upon a large complex of stucco buildings and a few shacks forming a horseshoe. This was Division Headquarters, forward. The Jeep stopped in front of the Intelligence Shop. I followed Wilkey inside. The people said "hello" to him. They just glanced at me. I was a strange face.

This is Captain Zonderman from Division Legal. He'll be prosecuting that rape case.

The suspicious faces loosened up. The gunnery sergeant's face flickered to life.

Oh yes. What can we do, Sir?

I'd like to use Chan for a couple of hours. I've got to interview some witnesses.

The 'Gunny' told Corporal Landers to go outside and see if he can find Chan. I smiled. The transition was almost humorous. The moment they found out I was prosecuting, all kinds of doors opened. There would be complete cooperation. When Barnard came poking around, they would know he was the enemy, poor bastard.

The corporal came back in. Trailing behind him was a tall, chubby, smiling Vietnamese young man, a rarity. Chan was told to go along with me to the village to help interview people involved in that rape last week. "You remember that rape last week?" "Oh yeah," Chan said still smiling. "I remember. Bad scene. Number 10, Dai-wee."

After leaving the camp and driving about a kilometer through the woods, they entered a small clearing containing about a dozen grass huts. Chan jumped out of the Jeep without a word. He made his way to one of the huts, and talked with an old man, the Village Chief, sitting in front of it in the shade. I could see them talking and gesturing. Then Chan sauntered back to us and said, "He say old women out in field. Girl at her father's house. He send for her."

I lit a cigarette as we followed Chan into the woods. Then I saw a water buffalo lurking behind one of the huts. I kept my eye on him. They always made me nervous. They got fidgety around Americans. Often, they would charge like a bull. They could identify the scent of an American, much the way our German Shepherds could sense a Vietnamese.

After a few minutes, the old man approached with a young Vietnamese girl and another man. She was noticeably young and sweet looking. She'd be a good witness if I could get her to talk. Chan introduced them. "This is Miss Nguyen and her father." I said, "Tell them that I am very sorry she was injured." I watched the girl and her father as Chan interpreted. Then the father spoke, and Chan said:

He say he want to know if you come to pay him.

I replied, tell him we are here to discuss his daughter's attack. We are here to punish the Marine. We do not want him to go away unpunished, but to do this we must know exactly what happened. She must tell us. Tell her I understand that she may be embarrassed, but we must know exactly what happened.

The girl looked us all over while Chan was translating. She was shy, but proud and angry. Her demeanor was different from that of her father. It was not humble fear. She looked us all in the eye.

The interview was a bit difficult, but she did fill me in on the general picture. I decided not to press for too many details in the initial interview. All I needed at this time was probable cause that a rape had been committed so that a General Court Martial would be convened. The physician's testimony would tend to show intercourse. My immediate goal was only to gain her confidence and cooperation.

I told Chan to tell her that we will have a vehicle here to bring them to the camp on Thursday at ten o'clock. The girl glared at us and spoke softly.

> She say she very mad at Americans. They say Americans come to help. You don't help. Look what they do.

When the girl was through speaking, I spoke briefly with one of the women who was in the dump. She described the attack:

> A black Marine had chased them. She saw him drag Nguyen into the bushes, tear her pajama pants off and get on top of her. Then the bodies went up and down.

I asked if the girl struggled. The woman said that "She did so at first but that the Marine was too big."

I said, "Fine." I'd like to talk with the other man with Gibson, what was his name? "Private Fuller," the lieutenant answered. "I'll send a man down to get him." It was time to break for lunch. When we returned to the PMO office, Private Fuller was waiting. He seemed quite nervous. I walked over to him.

> Well Captain, it's 'kinda' hard. Gibson is a friend of mine. I was there too, and I don't want any trouble.

Look, you didn't do anything wrong - - yet; and the only way you're going to get into trouble is if you hold out on me. And if you do that, you can't imagine what trouble is.

Yes, I guess so. When this whole mess started, I called my dad in Chu Lai. He's a gunnery sergeant. He told me the same thing, but I work and live with this guy, you know.

Look, if you're worried about reprisals, don't! I'll take care of that. We'll get you out of here. Listen, your father gave you some good advice. No reason for you to get in bad for something Gibson did. This is serious business.

Will Gibson know what I've said?

You'll have to testify at the Court Martial. You were a witness, and nothing can change that, but like I said, I'll take care of you. Besides, you are going to testify - - one way or another. I suggest that you take your dad's advice and tell the truth - - no more, no less.

I sensed that Fuller wasn't convinced. I decided to play my trump card.

Listen, Fuller, if you don't show me that you are with me, I'm going to figure you're against me. I may just conclude that you are withholding evidence, or maybe you were an accessory.

No Sir. I had nothing to do with no rape.

Look, I just want you to tell the truth and play it straight. It's as simple as that.

I felt a little bad. It was not fun to bully people. I could understand this man's anxiety. The comradeship was commendable, but this was a little different from the normal situation. I knew Fuller had not been part of the rape, so he had no right to remain silent.

Why don't we sit down, I said, gesturing to a couple of empty chairs? Let's start at the beginning.

Well, Sir, we were on detail up at the dump when we saw these three Gooks. We ran after them, kinda screaming, trying to scare them off. We stopped at the fenced edge of the dump. Then Gibson went after the girl. I saw him grab the little Gook and kind of drag her down a gully. That's it, we just went about our business.

Did you see Gibson again?

Yes, Sir. He came back about fifteen minutes later.

Did he say anything to you?

Fuller paused shifting in his chair. I leaned toward him.

Well, what did he say, man?

Fuller shifted in his chair again.

He said that she had struggled a lot, but he finally got her. She was tight, but nice.

Did you say anything to him?

Fuller squirmed in the chair and said: "No Sir."

You mean he told you he had just raped this girl and you didn't say anything?

No, Sir, we just laughed.

OK, is there anything else you can tell me? I asked in a voice which I hoped lacked any judgmental quality.

No, Sir.

That will be all for now. No one will know what we've talked about. Don't you say anything to Gibson. Play it like you know from nothing. If another captain comes around from Division Legal, just answer his questions truthfully, but don't volunteer anything, and if you can avoid him, well just play it cool. I don't think that I'll need you for the Article 32. That should keep your life easy around here for a while. If you're concerned about testifying at the trial, I'll try to get you a grant of immunity, so that you don't have to worry about the women implicating you. You know what I'm talking about?

No Sir, not really.

OK, it's a letter from the Commanding General which grants you an immunity from prosecution in this matter if you testify. Although you have a duty to testify, I'll get this for you as insurance because your father's an old timer, and because you're cooperating.

After Fuller left, I told the lieutenant,

I think that just about wraps it up for now. I'll come up in the morning on Thursday. Arrange with the Village Chief to have the three women and the girl ready about 10 AM. Also have the doctor, the sergeant from the dump, all standing by. Oh yeah, please arrange to have Chan there. That's a must. If you run into any problems on that give me a call down at Phu Bai.

I looked at my watch and decided that if I hurried, I could catch a flight back to Phu Bai.

It was no surprise that the Article 32 investigation found adequate evidence to refer the matter to a General Court Martial. The charges were prepared, and it was time to set a trial date. That was done by getting on the phone to Danang where the III MAF (3rd Marine Amphibious Force) Law Officer was located. He was like a Circuit Judge who would preside at the trial, and his schedule determined the trial date.

The date was set in three weeks. Now I started my actual trial preparation. I went through their few dogeared dusty books checking the laws on rape and other possible evidentiary issues. There were several administrative problems which had to be taken care of. I had to arrange the transportation and billeting of my witnesses. The military personnel were no problem, but the Vietnamese could not stay on the Phu Bai base overnight. The decision was reached that they would be billeted in a hotel in Hue at government expense. I was also able to procure three cartons of C rations for them and arrange for Chan to come down early with the villagers.

The day finally came when they were to arrive. I got one of the enlisted men to drive me down to the airstrip in a small pickup truck. We arrived just as the C-130 was setting down at Phu Bai. Three Vietnamese women clad in black pajamas and straw hats disembarked. With their little baskets and disoriented manner, they looked like lost souls. Right behind them was Lt. Wilkey and the girl's father. I approached them, smiled, and bowed. "Chan, tell them I'm happy to see them. Then take them over to the truck," I said, pointing to their vehicle. I then thanked Lt. Wilkey for bringing them down to Phu Bai. "No sweat captain. Just nail that bastard, Gibson," he replied.

I loaded them all onto the truck headed for Hue. It was one of only three real cities in South Vietnam, along with Danang and Saigon. It was the 'ancient capital' and was off-limits for Marines without authorized business. The first stop was the police station, near the hotel. The local police refused to allow the Vietnamese to enter the city. I had Chan explain the reason for their stay, but the police still refused. Then I had to make numerous phone calls. Finally, I contacted the local Vietnamese Army Commander, and everything was settled.

When we got to the hotel, everything went smoothly. Chan told me how many piasters were required to pay for the room. After they were registered, I took them upstairs. The room was simple.

Although this would be considered a 'flop house' in the States, it was quite luxurious for Vietnam. It even had a toilet. The women had never lived so fancy. They were dirt floor, grass shack people from up North. It was quite exciting for them.

When they were all settled, I had Chan tell them that they were on their own until the next morning at eight o'clock when I would send someone to pick them up. I had Chan advise them to stay close to the hotel. I took out a few piasters and put them on the table. It seemed that there was so little I could do for them.

I spent the following day reviewing their testimony with them back at the camp. I interviewed them individually and as a group, going over the questions that I or the defense counsel might ask. Through repetition, I hoped to familiarize them with the format of the trial. This might help to relax them. As they went over the stories, they gained confidence. The greatest problem was the girl's testimony. She would fill in everything except the details of the rape.

> She say that he pull her into the bushes, pull off her pants, and rape her.

> Tell her that the word 'rape' is a conclusion. She must tell me exactly what he did with his body and hers.

> Go outside and get her father, I requested.

When the two returned, I spoke to the father.

> Tell her not to be embarrassed. We cannot punish the man who did this to her unless she tells us exactly what happened.

While the father was speaking to the daughter, I turned my attention to Chan and the others in the room.

> There is no place for smiles. I want you to look serious. This is very embarrassing for the girl. Okay Chan, the father is finished. Let's try it again. Tell her that we are

> all adults, and that we are all here to help her. We want to punish this man. You just tell us exactly how it happened.

> She say that he pull her into bushes. Then he take off her pajama bottoms. Then his own pants. Then he got on top of her. Then he rape me.

> Oh no, I mumbled under my breath.

> OK. Let's try it another way. Ask her this. After he did what he did, what parts of her body hurt. What did she feel?

> She say, her pussy hurt, Chan announced in a voice loud enough to be heard through the office.

I glanced at the girl. She was looking around, mortified. I felt bad for her. But, perhaps, it could be salvaged. It might have been lucky that it happened now, when I had an opportunity to rehabilitate her spirits, rather than tomorrow in the courtroom. I turned my attention to Chan.

> Chan, you have got to use the right words. I am going to teach them to you, and I want you to use them from now on. The proper word for 'pussy' is 'vagina'. On the male, it's called a 'penis'. Tell her that this is what she needs to know to punish this man.

> She say she understand. She will do.

For the next half hour, I tried to get the simple but necessary statement from the girl. Finally, she did it, and Chan relayed it using the proper vocabulary.

> Fine. Look Chan, I think she's had it for now. I'd like to have you stay with them in Hue tonight. She's still a little shaky. Try to reassure her and go over some of the questions like we did today. The more familiar it is, the less embarrassing it will be to her, and to all of them.

The day had finally come. The Law Officer flew up to Phu Bai. Word was out that there would be a General Court Martial. There was noticeable tension in the camp. Groups were hanging around the courtroom hut.

I went over to check the room and make sure that everything was being set up. In the back, there were a few benches for observers. In the front, there was a long table and chairs where the members of the Court Martial panel (jury) would sit. There was a pitcher of water and some glasses, and a copy of the charges for each member. Copies were placed on the desk and chair of each counsel. There was also a table where the Court Reporters sat with their equipment.

I went back to the office for last minute preparations. I was relieved when Chan came in and told me that the witnesses were outside eating their breakfast of C-rations, and that they were ready. I called Private Fuller into the office, gave him the Grant of Immunity document signed by the Commanding General, and asked if he was all set. Fuller replied that he had one problem: it would be awkward going back to his base camp at Dong Ha. I responded that I would see if I could get him a transfer.

As ten o'clock came closer, I walked over to the Courtroom. I didn't know what defense Captain Barnard would come up with, but Bill was a sharp and worthy opponent.

I went outside to smoke a cigarette. At 10:00 am, the Law Officer arrived at the Courtroom. It took a few minutes for everybody to take their proper seats. The Law Officer asked me if I was ready. I replied that I was, and the Law Officer called the Court to order.

After the formalities were dispensed with, I started presenting my case. The first few witnesses had testified as I had expected them to. The sergeant from the dump testified about the girl's complaint and her physical appearance at the time. The attending physician testified that there had been penetration and sperm found inside the vagina indicating recent intercourse. I asked him if he had an opinion as to her virginity prior to this incident. The doctor said it was only an opinion, but that recent tears in the membrane might lead to that conclusion. On cross-examination by Bill Barnard, the doctor replied that it was his educated opinion, based upon his examination and training, that she had been a virgin. Bill backed off before any more damage was done.

Private Fuller's testimony was not seriously challenged on cross-examination. The two women both testified with ease and confidence. Barnard could not shake their stories. The only possible point Barnard made was why they didn't try to help or run for assistance, and they answered they were scared.

I then called Lieutenant Jerry Wilkey, who did the initial investigation and conducted the lineup. When I asked Wilkey to describe the lineup and the results, Barnard jumped up and objected, waving a piece of paper in his hand. I wondered what he had up his sleeve. The Law officer asked, what was the nature of Barnard's objection?

> When this lineup was held, my client was without counsel. This is a violation of his constitutional rights as set forth in the Supreme Court Case of <u>United States v. Wade</u>.[2]

The Law Officer said that we'd better go into an out-of-court hearing, and he recessed the proceedings. I was taken completely by surprise and wondered where Barnard had gotten this recent case from. I then asked for a brief recess. Barnard had no objection, so a thirty-minute recess was granted. I walked over to Bill and said,

> Where the Hell did you get that case? It wasn't in the law books available in the office. Give, it can't hurt. The issue has already been raised.

> Well, if you must know, I wrote to some Civil Rights groups when I got the case. They sent me some material and The Wade case was in there. Sorry, pal. Just doing the best I can to protect my client's rights.

---

2 388 US at 218 (1967)

I decided to go over to the Legal Office to see if the colonel knew anything about <u>Wade.</u>

> Well, Zonderman, what are you going to do about this Wade case?

> Well, Sir. I'm not really sure. I'd like to read it first if I can find it in any of our materials.

As I walked out of the Colonel's office, I saw Major Linnehan chuckling.

> Look Paul, I have something I want you to look at, and he handed me some sheets of paper. The Law Officer down in Danang has a better law library and is up on this stuff. He brought this material up with him. Take a quick look at it and then bring it right back.

As I scanned the papers, my eyes stopped on one section. It was all that I needed. I copied down a few sentences and returned the papers to the major.

Back in the courtroom, The Law Officer came in and took his seat.

> The out-of-court hearing will come to order. Let the record show that the Court has withdrawn from the courtroom; present are the trial and defense counsels, the accused, Law Officer, and reporters. This hearing will be marked as Appellate Exhibit 1 and inserted at this point in the record.

I sat back and listened to Bill's eloquent argument on his client's constitutional rights. As he sat down, he grinned at me. The Law Officer turned to me, "Is there anything that you'd like to say?"

> Yes, Sir, there is. Although I share Defense Counsel's great respect for the safeguards enumerated in the 6th Amendment, I am sorry to say that the decision in <u>Wade</u> was held not to apply retroactively in the case of Stovall

v. Denno[3]. The lineup which concerns us was conducted prior to the <u>Wade</u> decision and therefore does not come under that rule of law. I also hasten to add that when the victim later identifies the accused, it will be as a result of her clear view of him on the date of the offense, and not because of any pre-trial lineups.

I grinned at Bill and sat down. Bill glanced at the Law Officer and then back at me with an unfriendly look in his eyes.

Objection Overruled. Will one of you go out and tell the court that we will be reconvening.

The panel re-entered the courtroom and the Law Officer called the Court to order. I could now introduce the lineup testimony.

I recall Lt. Wilkey.
Now Lieutenant, you testified that you conducted a lineup in the course of your investigation. Would you please describe for us exactly how this took place?

On the 26th of April, at about ten o'clock in the morning, Sgt. Holman from my office went to some quarters near the PMO headquarters and selected four young black males between five feet nine inches and six feet tall. He chose men who neither had very dark nor light complexions. They were brought back to our area where they were assembled in a line against the wall of our headquarters building. Fuller was number one on the right. Gibson was second in from the left. At this point the victim was brought outside from one of the other buildings at a point where she could easily observe all the men. She was instructed to look them over very carefully before she made any identification, and to tell the interpreter which man raped her, if any. She picked the second man from the left, who was Gibson."

---

3 388 US at 293 (6-12-67)

And you were present when all this took place?

Yes.

How was it that defendant was in this lineup?

I had developed him as a suspect.

Under what circumstances?

He was one of the two black Marines on dump detail that morning.

On cross-examination, Barnard established that there was prostitution in Dong Ha, including sixteen-year-old girls, who tried to sell themselves to the Marines. I realized that this was going to be Barnard's defense, to show that this was a voluntary financial affair gone wrong.

I then called the victim, Nguyen Thi Nguyen, to testify. It was established who she was, where she lived, and that she was at the dump on the day in question with two older ladies. She described the situation as follows:

> She was at the trash dump at Dong Ha with some older women. A Marine chase and grab her. After the Marine catch her, he drag her down to ground and rape her.

I asked her to describe what parts of his body touched her body and where did she hurt.

> She say she had pajama shirt and pants on. He push her on ground; he pull off her pants. She kick and punch, but he too big and much strong. She say he put his penis in her vagina. Then he run away. She was sore in back and vagina. She bleed and cry much. Plenty mad, Her friends come to help her.

Ms. Nguyen, would you recognize the Marine who did this to you?

While I waited for the translation, I looked over at the defense table. I was astounded to see that four similar looking black defendants were slipped into the courtroom and sitting at the defense table with Gibson. Very clever. I turned back to Chan.

Ask her if she recognizes the man who did this to her.

She say, yes. She will not forget that face.

Ask if the person who did this to her is in the courtroom, will she walk over at point at him?

The girl got up and walked over to the defense table. I walked by her side. The members of the Board knew this was crucial. Finally, she pointed at Gibson. I stepped between them, just in case. She sat down. It was now time for Barnard's cross-examination.

Ask her if it is true that she was at the dump so that she could sell herself.

Her voice was angry. No translation was necessary. She say no. She good girl. He rape her.

Isn't it true that he paid her and that they argued because she wanted more?

She say no, no. He rape her. She fight with him. You only try to protect this man.

No more questions.

The prosecution rests, I said with relief.

Gibson exercised his right not to take the stand and the testimony was over. The summations were brief. I just reviewed the facts. Barnard just argued consent, gone wrong. The Law Officer gave his instructions to the Court and then they recessed.

It was a half hour later when the court was ready to come in with a verdict. When everyone was in his seat, the court was called to order. I said, "Let the record show that all parties present when the court recessed are again present. Bill and I stood up facing the Court. The President of the Court looked over at us for a moment and then started to read from a paper before him.

> Private David Gibson, it is my duty as president of this court to inform you that the court in closed session and upon secret written ballot two thirds of the members present at the time the vote was taken, concurring in the finding, finds you: Of the Specification of the Charge, GUILTY.
>
> We will now hear argument on the sentence. Captain Barnard, you may begin.

Barnard simply referred to Gibson's record and the strain of combat. Although he had been found guilty of rape, the girl still might have tempted him.

This was a contrast to his usual eloquent style. I began my argument on sentencing.

> Gentlemen, here we have a young, pretty girl who has been attacked. Apart from the instant when the rape took place, there will be side effects which will linger forever. The trauma and the humiliation will remain. We will have to go a long way to change the negative feelings of this girl and her neighbors. Their eyes are upon us to see that we do not condone this inexcusable conduct. Gibson is no less culpable because it was committed here and now. It should be dealt with in the same manner as the rape of any young girl in the United States. The punishment should be fixed accordingly.

Another short panel recess was called for deliberation. When they came back in, the President of the Court announced the sentence:

Private David Gibson, it is my duty as President of this court to inform you that the court in closed session and upon a secret written ballot, two thirds of the members present at the time the vote was taken concurring, sentence you: to be dishonorably discharged from the service, forfeit all pay and allowances, be reduced to pay grade E-1, and to be confined at hard labor for a term of five years.

I was stunned. Only five years for rape. Anywhere else he would have gotten twenty. It was hypocrisy. Weren't her rights worth the same as an American girl. If that's the way they feel, what are we doing here.

I turned quickly as I heard some scuffling to my right. Gibson began to jump across his desk and lunge at me. I went over backwards in my chair as my desk was knocked over. Gibson was quickly restrained by two MP's.

After the trial, I walked back to my hootch in Phu Bai and sat alone in silence. It was a tough case with a tough opponent.

TEN

TALKING POLITICS

I had managed to drive the monsoon season out of my mind and clothing, and I was now learning to tolerate the hot season. It had come upon us quickly. One evening, as I was leaving the "O" Club, I realized that I had left my flashlight behind. What surprised me was that, for some reason, I didn't need it - - I could see where I was walking. This confused me because it was usually so pitch black at night. I looked around. This world was brighter than I could ever recall seeing it. And then I saw them: stars in the sky. There was even a moon. I realized what had happened: the solid cloud cover of the rainy season had finally broken up.

Soon, I realized that the beauty of the stars and moon was no consolation in the 130-degree heat of mid-day. Instead of being wet, damp, and cold, I found myself sweat-soaked and dirty. The dust stuck to you. *So did the mysterious stuff that they sprayed down on you from helicopters, supposedly to clear the foliage around the camp[4]*

The Danang PX began to stock electric fans and small Japanese refrigerators. Soda was sold by the case. You had to replace the fluids which poured out of you. Utility shirts were chopped to short sleeves. Even inside the Legal Hut, in front of the fans, it was 110 degrees. It was hard to think abstractly in heat like that. There was just no comfortable season.

One day, as I was being driven by the Staff area, I recognized an old friend, and told the driver to stop. I jumped out and walked over to a man and tapped him on the shoulder. Everett turned, his face lighting up in a big smile. "Paul, it's great to see you. I asked for you at Division Legal. They told me you were out on some claims investigation. Tell you what. I'll stick around for a couple of days. How about meeting at the club tonight?" "Great," I said with enthusiasm.

That evening, the two of us met at the "O" Club. After I had filled Everett in on what I had been doing, I asked the same of Everett. He told me of one incident he was involved in down in Ple Ku which might interest me.

> One of the gunships was called into a firefight. When they got there, they observed a figure running from emplacement to emplacement. Well, the Crew Chief cut it down with his machine gun. The fight ended quickly, and they went down to confirm the KIA's. Well, it seems that the figure he opened up on was a pregnant woman. The Vietnamese raised some flack and the foreign press got hold of it. They labelled him a psychopathic killer. That wouldn't have been so bad until the fat cats in Danang got involved. Some high-echelon asshole sitting in an air-conditioned office down there decided that an investigation was in order. Well, then it really hit the fan. You

---

4 Agent Orange, See EPILOG

know how the men in the field love those chopper crews. They raised all kinds of smoke. A couple of high-ranking enlisted men interceded and the whole thing was squelched. I'll tell you that I spoke to the Crew Chief And his pilot. They were pretty pissed off.

I know. I haven't had any cases like that yet, but many of the old timers have. The poor guy in the action is caught in the middle between giants.

That would be a good name for a story. "The Battle of the Giants," that's exactly what it is. On the one side, you have the colonel in charge of combat operations G-2 telling them to kill. On the other side, you have the G-5 colonel in charge of pacification who is concerned with our image.

Yeah, he tells them to make love, not war, I interjected.

Everett's face became serious.

But seriously Paul, these kids are in a hell of a bind. The politics filters right down through the jungle onto that bloody square foot of earth that he's fighting on and sometimes dying for. Hell, sometimes they don't even know who the enemy is. If they make a mistake and kill a civilian, they get Court Martialed.

I know Ev. There was a good cartoon on that in the Army Times a few weeks ago. It had this young private and a grizzly old sergeant walking through a village. The private looked kind of nervous. He looks up at the sergeant and asks, "How can you tell the friendlies from the enemies?" The sergeant replies: "The enemy is the one who is shooting at you." Sometimes that's too late. It's like trying to distinguish between a Democrat and a Republican.

Everett shifted himself in the chair. I could tell that he was getting upset. Ev went on.

You know the situations are classic. At the simplest level, you have a youngster who sees his buddy blown to bits when some meek looking little farmer reaches into his basket and lobs a grenade into a passing military truck. The next day he sees another meek little farmer reach into his basket, act suspicious, and begin to draw out something dark and round. Fearing another grenade attack, he fires instinctively, killing the farmer. Come to find out, he was only reaching for a piece of fruit, perhaps to offer to the troops. Now a friendly villager is dead. It's tragic. Then begins the battle of giants. Perhaps the Commanding General has just re-emphasized the political importance of our good image. Then you boys take over because you investigate and possibly convene a General Court Martial.

Don't blame it on us. We have to defend or prosecute these guys. You know it goes beyond the generals. You can't fight a guerilla war to suit the sensibilities of an uninvolved television audience at home. They let the photographers and reporters travel with some of the units. Newscasters and reporters bury the public with the hot news. The more you watch or read about a war, one you don't understand in the first place, the more you dislike it as well as the soldiers involved who are coming home.

There is another example I'll share with you. It happened just a couple of days ago. I was walking near the command area, and everybody was standing at attention and saluting while our national anthem was playing. The Vietnamese day workers in the area also stood at attention. The music then began to play the Vietnamese national anthem. We all stayed at attention, but the Vietnamese just walked away. They either didn't know that it was their national anthem, or they didn't care. Except in a few established cities like Saigon, or Danang, or Hue, there is no real sense of government out here where the fighting takes place. These aren't your fat cats in Saigon getting rich from the war.

These people just want to be let alone to raise their families and rice. The munitions and defoliants certainly don't help.

Everett brought up another issue. He told me that he was almost finished with an article on marijuana usage and asked if we had any problems with that up here. I replied,

I've been on both sides in those cases. Everyone in our office has been involved. It got to the point that we stopped handling them with Court Martials and began using Administrative Hearings. You may be familiar with the smell, taste, and appearance of marijuana, but you need a lab analysis to get a conviction. In a Court Martial case, that means that you either bring the lab witness from Japan, or you send the opposing counsels to Japan to take his deposition. If I am defending, I can object to the introduction of lab analysis without the expert present, even if I know the procedure is usually valid. So, I go in to the major and say that I want the government to spend the money to bring the lab technician here or send counsel to Japan to depose him.

The office major usually reacts with something like: You young punk. You son of a bitch. What are you trying to pull? You know the chemist is an expert. You're also a military officer with a duty not to put the command through unnecessary expense.

It's a difficult situation. You want to do the best for your client. You want your boss to be pleased when you do a good job. You are morally obligated to protect your client's interests and hold the government to compliance with the undisputed rules of evidence. These are the client's safeguards, not loopholes that you ignore. So, the lawyers were called in for a conference. Our asses got reamed. We were told that whoever continued making trouble would be sent up to Dong Ha to provide legal aid for the troops on the DMZ. In fact, one of us was sent up to Dong Ha. I guess the brass knew they were at fault here, so a practical solution was ultimately arrived at. No more Court Martials for marijuana. They would be handled in an Administrative Hearing where the rules of evidence are not applied, and the penalty is much less severe: general or undesirable discharge, and no fines or imprisonment involved.

Everett replied that marijuana is a real problem. It's so easy to get here, and the pressures the men are under may cause a lot of guys to use it; and don't forget, our good friends, the South Vietnamese, are making a lot of money on it.

By the way, have you heard that we are retiring those old heavy M-14's?

Oh yeah. I just had a chance to test out one of the new ones recently. A few weeks ago, I was in the North country. This particular unit had just been issued the new M-16's and they were in the process of testing them out on a makeshift range. I walked over to watch, and the lieutenant asked me if I'd like to try one. Naturally, I said yes. Compared to the old heavy wooden M-14, these are a dream. They are light and easy to fire. You can actually aim them. In fact, I put one on fully automatic and rested the butt on my forehead, and let a few rounds go. It was painless and easy. With the old M-14 on fully automatic, you could barely hold on to it. I told the lieutenant the M-16 was great. He then told me that their sister Battalion had been given the M-16's two weeks ago, and they took them out into the boonies, and they got clobbered. The guns were jamming, and there were a lot of dead Marines found with their cleaning rods still in the barrel. So, the remedy was to run a couple of hundred rounds through the M-16 which loosened it up and then they worked fine. This platoon I was visiting was doing just that.

"It gets depressing when you think about it. So how are things at home? Is the baby born yet," Everett inquired? "The baby should be coming soon. There are still happy things in this world."

ELEVEN

THE RED CROSS

Weeks had passed and I was constantly aware that Ann could deliver at any time now. My father had arranged with the Red Cross to inform them when the baby came, and they in turn would immediately send a telegram to me. They were given the name and location of my unit to expedite the message. I was surprised to learn that the Red Cross kept a couple of agents in one of the shacks in the area to link to the stateside communication network. We had an ID number so that the Boston office could expedite the message. The Red Cross agent that I had befriended was Marty Green. I was impressed that Red Cross civilians would live in this area. Mortar attacks were still common here and would increase in the better weather. I kept in touch with Marty.

On May 16, 1967, when I was somewhere out in the countryside, a person in green fatigues with a red cross emblem tapped me on the shoulder. It was Marty. He handed me a telegram style message. I read the words and broke out in a big smile. "Mother and daughter doing fine." That's what I wanted to hear. My eyes filled with tears. Good girl, Ann. I didn't know what to do. I felt like jumping up and down. Then I realized I had to get cigars to hand out in the office.

This would be a new hat for me to wear: husband, son, lawyer, Marine, and now father. I was becoming 'saltier' in that tour of duty we call a lifetime. If only I could start to meet those responsibilities now. God, I didn't even know what she looked like. I hoped I would get a picture soon. I looked up at Marty and said, "Thanks." Marty smiled warmly.

It's nothing. Look, we usually inform you orally. I tore that sheet right off the ticker tape. We're supposed to keep them. But, well, I thought you might want to save it.

I'll save it. Don't worry. God, Marty, I'm a father. I'll share this joy with anyone.

Congratulations, Pop. Well, I've got to get back to work.

Thanks again, Marty, I really appreciate it.

That's why I do it.

I sat there, re-reading the telegram which did not state the baby's name. I thought a girl would be named Lauren Jean as we had decided upon together. Ann changed the Jean to Jo which was an affectionate part of my grandmother's nickname. She must have thought that would please me. The letter about naming her Lauren Jo arrived a few weeks after she was born.

I returned to the legal shack to hand out the cigars in a casual manner. I didn't really have any close friends, although I liked and respected several of the guys. They were happy for me.

That evening, I saw Everett as soon as he walked into the Officers Club. I handed him a couple of cigars without a word. Everett's face opened up into a big grin. "Paul, that's great. Was it a boy or a girl?" "A girl." "What's her name?" "Lauren."

The world looked different. It was a little bigger and more beautiful. My daughter had been added. Later that night, I expressed my joy in a tape to Ann.

```
VZCZCVPA172MCA046
PP RUMNVP
DE RUEDJPA3131 1351702
ZNR UUUUU
P 151924Z MAY 67
FM AMCROSS WASHDC
TO AMCROSS 3RD MARDIV PHU BAI VN
ARX GRNC
BT
UNCLAS MSG 3166 RPT MSG 3166 FM CHAPT NEWTON MASS
RE CAPT PAUL S ZONDERMAN 086020 HQS BN  HQS CO DIV LEGAL 3RD MARDIV
FPO SF 96602  DR  ZONDERMAN FATHER OF OFFICER REQUEST YOU INFORM
HIM WIFE ANN DELIVERED BEAUTIFUL BABY GIRL THIS DATE MAY 15 6 LBS
14 OZS 20 INCHES LONG MOTHER AND BABY FINE
BT
```

I received this message
on 16 May 1967 at 0800
at Phu Bai, VIETNAM

P. S. ZONDERMAN
Capt 086020 USMCR

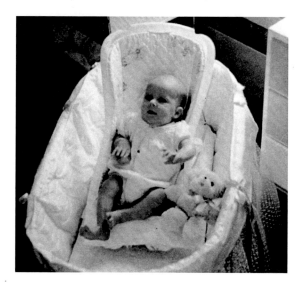

TWELVE

REST AND RECUPERATION (R & R)

As midyear 1967 was approaching, I began checking with Company Headquarters as to when my R&R flight to Hawaii showed up on the manifest. The continual "Not yet, Sir" had ruined each day from the start. Other services gave their men two or three R&R breaks. Apparently, the Marines only needed one. I could have selected Hong Kong or Thailand, but Hawaii was the best place to meet Ann. Then, one day when I entered, the Top Sergeant looked up from his desk and said the magic words: "The manifest is in, Sir. You're on it. Next Tuesday."

My first task was to call Ann via a ham radio phone patch (Military Amateur Radio System) and give her the date. I was able to get through to a ham in California, who made the phone call to her in Boston. When her voice came over the crackling line, it dazzled my brain and I hesitated for a moment. I kept the conversation brief and unemotional partly because the radio signals could cut out at any time and partly because I was at a loss for words. I gave her the date, the time, and the flight number of my arrival in Hawaii. The call just emphasized to me how far away I was from my wife and child.

In the days that followed, I busied myself getting my gear together. I took a beat up set of khakis from my hot box and made a mental note to have one of the mama-sans iron it. Except for my shirt and fatigues, that was all the clothes I would take. Ann would bring some for me to wear in Hawaii.

The day before my departure, I went down to Danang to stay overnight in transient quarters. I purchased an 8mm movie projector in the PX there, to view movies of Lauren that Ann was bringing to Hawaii. The excitement was beginning to build up. Danang was a noisy place because the fighter jets were constantly taking off and landing. The screeching sound was quite loud. When I woke up in the morning, I learned that I had slept through a rocket attack on Danang. I checked myself for shrapnel. No problem.

I checked into the air terminal at 0600. After many delays, a big Pan American jet taxied in front of the terminal. It looked beautiful. I boarded the craft with the others and settled back in a seat. I'd relax when it was up in the sky and bullets from below couldn't reach me. I felt out of place in a luxury plane. Would my wife find me a stranger? After a flight that seemed like it would never end, the plane set down in Hawaii. I was in the United States. I knew I should feel thrilled, but over the previous six months I had trained myself not to feel.

The Marines shuffled along in line with blank expressions as they disembarked. Stepping inside the terminal, I noticed a glass wall to the left. Behind it I saw wives jumping and waiving. I also saw several Chaplains mixing with the crowd. They were there to console the wives whose husbands didn't make it. Their husbands or sons had become part of the statistic that one out of four Marines in Vietnam was either killed or wounded.

Then I recognized Ann in the crowd. I stopped and smiled slowly lifting my hand in a little waive. I watched her as I walked along. I was here. I made it. The customs procedure was brief. I was only asked if I had any weapons or explosives. I said, "No," so they didn't bother to open my bag. I was outside now. Ann threw her arms around me. We kissed briefly. As I gazed at her, I felt the warmth rising in me and it began to humanize me. I wanted to be alone with her, away from the crowds, but we were not allowed to leave with our families yet. We were first required to be bussed to the nearby R&R Center, where we would sign in. Ann followed the bus in a bright red Chevy which she had rented. I felt proud of her. She had come all this way and taken care of all the details.

At the R&R center, after the soldiers were seated, a lieutenant told the men how to fill out the cards. We were also cautioned not to talk about any confidential material. The lieutenant closed with, "Gentlemen, you are home now. Don't be animals anymore. Save it for when you go back," and then dismissed us. We scrambled for the doors.

I walked to Ann standing outside the R&R center. We kissed briefly, tears in both of our eyes, and walked quickly into the parking lot. As we approached the car, she asked me if I wanted to drive. It was nice for her to ask. I was her man - - her husband. "No thank you; I feel a little disoriented."

The car seemed so luxurious - - comfortable seats, roll-up windows, no bumps or dust or rain. As we pulled out of the parking lot, I relaxed, and Ann started talking. I responded briefly from time to time, but I really couldn't focus on conversation. It was like a strange dream, and I expected to be awakened by the hut doors slamming in the darkness, but I was with the woman I loved.

We pulled into the parking lot of a fancy hotel. Ann took me by the hand and led me through the hotel lobby into the elevator. All the faces seemed so friendly and expressive as if welcoming me. It was like being on your honeymoon and advertising it.

Once inside the room, I walked all around it, taking everything in. The bathroom looked so clean and modern. There was a good supply of toilet paper. I would not have to worry about insects or rats here. We walked outside onto the balcony into the warm night air. The lights were twinkling along the shore. What a beautiful temporary home this room would be.

Back in the room, we slowly started to unwind. Ann started to talk about the baby. There was so much to tell me. She showed me the newest photographs of Lauren. As I went through them, I just stared without comment, but a warm smile came over my face. I then asked to see the movies. Ann got the film reels and I set up the projector.

We lay on the bed holding hands while the wall was lit up with pictures of our child. Ann kept bouncing up with enthusiasm as she narrated the film. It bound us together. I listened to her commentary as I met my daughter vicariously. Together, we laughed, we talked, we loved.

The next morning, I awoke gradually. It was noon time. I looked at Ann asleep next to me. I wanted to wake her up, but she looked so peaceful. Instead, I got up and took a long shower. When I returned from the bathroom, she was sitting up in bed.

Good morning.

Yes it is, and I walked over and kissed her.

I'm starved. I need some good old home-style food.

There's a good restaurant downstairs. You'll find some clothes in the top drawer. I thought you had drowned in that hot shower.

Oh, I said. You couldn't believe how great hot water felt. I had a half a year of filth to wash off.

In the restaurant, I sat for a long time looking at the menu. The waitress came back a few times to take our order, but Ann waived her off. I felt like a boy in a candy store. Then, I decided to order several items including a cheeseburger, French fries, fresh fruit, and vegetables + + +. It was a feast.

After breakfast, as we were walking down a street, a pneumatic drill started up close to my rear. Instinctively, I hit the ground. Almost immediately, I realized where I was and recovered myself. I bounced right up, trying to make it look like I had merely tripped. I felt terribly self-conscious and embarrassed. Ann said nothing. She just held my arm tightly as we walked on, glad to turn the corner of the street. Tears welled up in my eyes. I loved her so much. I felt anger. What was I ashamed of? Didn't they know there was a war on, and I was part of it? Life was so cheap. Nobody here seemed to think about it. Perhaps it was thousands of miles away, but for me, it was only a few days until I would be back there again. Any veteran would have understood. "What's the matter," Ann asked. "Oh, nothing. My mind was just a few thousand miles away."

I wanted to buy my daughter a present, her first one from her father. We came upon a clothing store which had bathing suits. I picked out a colorful bikini for Lauren Jo and one for Ann. We would tell her the whole story when she would be old enough to understand.

During those few days, we walked in stores, did sightseeing, swam in the ocean, lay on the sand in the sun, visited the sunken Arizona Memorial, and bought a supply of canned foods for me to take back with me. In time, we started to feel normal together, but this wasn't exactly a vacation. It was an R&R, a time for rest and recuperation. We both knew that I knew I would be returning soon, so I had to hold back just a bit. Ann was amazed at the food I purchased: canned tuna, canned spaghetti and meatballs, smoked oysters, canned fruit, and similar camping trip items. She asked me, "Will you eat all that stuff?" I looked at her with eyes that momentarily revealed a sad, far-away look. She said no more but walked a little closer to me.

Finally, it was the last night of a beautiful interlude. I knew that I was ready to go. It wasn't that I didn't treasure this time together, but I needed to get back to get this over so I could live a normal family life again. We faced it quietly, each in our own way. The last evening embraces lingered a little longer.

The next morning at the airport, we stood by the gate talking casually. I thought it would be harder for her. I was like a moth being drawn to a flame. I had to put on my emotional armor and move toward my fate. Finally, it was time to board. I kissed her hard and held her close. I didn't want to let go. Quickly, but gently, I disengaged myself, and smiled at my wife. As I walked away, I had to look back one more time. This might be the last time I would ever see her. I didn't really believe that, no one ever did. But it was possible, and I sensed it with a chill.

Seated on the plane, I held many emotions in my head. It was a lot for one person to handle. "God," I prayed, "Just let the next six months end quickly and safely so that I can go home again. I can't leave Ann alone, and I have to hold my daughter in my arms."

It was a long ride back to Danang. I was tired when we arrived, but I wanted to get a flight back to Phu Bai immediately, back to my hut, my job, and everything I knew. It had been six months; it was time to change my sheets.

THIRTEEN

THE CHARLES WOODLEY TRIAL

When I arrived at Phu Bai, the hut was empty. Everyone was probably at the Club. I decided to go to sleep immediately. I didn't want to talk to anyone. I felt sad. I placed my steel pot and flak jacket next to my cot just in case I needed them that evening . Charlie might just welcome me back with a mortar or a rocket attack.

The next morning, it took me a few minutes to re-orient myself. The other men smiled at me. They spoke very briefly and cheerfully. Most of them had been through it. They understood. The returnee was always quiet and depressed. They kidded me briefly. "Isn't it great to be back?" It would take a little time to patch up my protective cover.

After breakfast, a private came in from the colonel's office and said, "The old man wants to see you." I shuffled across the dust to the colonel's office. The colonel looked up as I entered. "Well captain, have a good R&R?" "Yes, Sir. Thank you, Sir. My wife brought some movies of our baby."

The colonel looked uncomfortable. He hadn't really wanted an answer. I had caught him off guard. "We have some new cases," he said abruptly. "I hope you are refreshed and ready to go to work." "Yes, Sir," I replied.

> This is a good one up North. Looks like it might go to a General Court Martial for first-degree murder. It's a hot one - - - the shooting of a prisoner by Sergeant Charles Woodley. The brass down South wants action. I'm sure you'll be able to handle it. I'm assigning you as defense

counsel. Steve will be trial counsel. Major Linnehan will fill you in. Drop everything else and concentrate on this one. That will be all.

Yes, Sir.

I had to go up North again around the DMZ, to the tent camp of a Battalion out in the woods. I grabbed a C-130 going to Dong Ha. There, a Jeep and driver took me from Dong Ha to the Battalion HQ. I walked into the CO's office tent where a colonel sat at a makeshift desk.

I'm here on the Charles Woodley case.

Sit down, captain.

From what I read about the case, he looks like an otherwise good Marine. He is a sergeant with a good record. He has two years of college. Can't we talk about this a bit?

The colonel paused, with a sad look on his face, and responded:

No, I'm afraid the word got down to the General at Danang. Another platoon went through the area and found a dead Vietnamese civilian with his arms fastened behind him by his shirt. He was lying in a grass hut, shot by a shotgun. They thought it was another Viet Cong atrocity, so they reported it to the brass at Danang.

I'd like to talk with my client. Is he still up here?

Yes, but once the paperwork is done, he'll be sent to the Brig at Danang.

I walked into the tent and introduced myself to Woodley. "I'm Captain Zonderman. I have been assigned as your defense counsel. I'm here to try and help you."

My first impression of Sergeant Woodley was that he was a nice looking young black man, soft-spoken, with an intelligent manner.

He had finished two years of college and was a sergeant E-5. He told me what happened.

> It was a typically hot day (130°). My platoon had been out in the field for several days. We were tired and exhausted. We had several encounters with the VC and our platoon of 40 was reduced to 30 men. We were patrolling through a 'free fire zone.' That is an area where all the friendly citizens have been temporarily evacuated by their government so that anyone present would be considered an enemy. The US troops were allowed to pass through. Somewhere in this 'free fire zone' we captured a middle-aged Vietnamese man. We didn't know what to do with him. We couldn't take him with us because he might try to give us away. If we tied him to a tree and left him, he might later be able to tell any VC that our platoon was weak and reduced in size. My commander was a young 2nd lieutenant who called the group together to give our opinion on what to do with the prisoner, 'thumbs up or thumbs down.' The group all gave a thumbs down. Then, the lieutenant ordered me to take him over to that hut (pointing) and blow him away. They had pulled the man's shirt down in a way that bound his arms to his sides. I hesitatingly walked the prisoner away from the group. I was behind the man and held his left elbow with my left hand. My right hand held my shotgun. I did not want to shoot this man, but I had an order from my commanding officer to do so. As I walked the prisoner, I feared that the man might be a judo expert, or he might be able to walk me into a punji pit. When we reached the hut and stopped at the entrance, the man whirled around (to plead?) and I instinctively stepped back and shot him.

That was the gist of Woodley's story. He never wanted to do it, but he was afraid of violating his lieutenant's orders. He repeated this story to me in several visits to the Danang Brig. He knew there was a Nuremberg rule out of World War II that following orders does not justify an unlawful act such as murder. He responded that he was afraid for his life under the circumstances and was defending himself. I knew that there were three possible defenses I could raise:

1. What was the real meaning of a Free Fire Zone if not to give the Marines the right to shoot any Vietnamese person in the designated area

2. Woodley shot in self-defense when the man whirled around and startled him.

3. He was obeying his commander's order in a combat situation, the violation of which could have him sent to prison. I knew that this would be an uphill battle, but I wanted very much to save this man.

At the General Court Martial trial, I wanted the Law Officer (Judge) to accept the above evidence and instruct the panel defenses that they could consider these as possible defenses. The act was not disputed. Woodley admitted it. Woodley then testified essentially that he was hesitant to shoot the man, but he followed the first part of the order to walk him away. He had the prisoner, but he was frightened of him. He stopped in front of the hut because he was afraid to go in. When the man whirled around, the shot was instinctive. There wasn't much for the panel to decide because the Law Officer would not allow me to present any of the three defenses. The panel thus came in with a guilty verdict. It was the sentence that really disturbed me: Dishonorable Discharge and thirty years in a Naval prison. I thought there was error here and a ground for appeal, and that the sentence was also extreme under the circumstances.

Then another issue came up. The young lieutenant in command would be prosecuted next, and the command wanted Woodley to testify against him. If he did, they told me they would reduce his sentence to twenty years. After discussion, Woodley decided he did not want to so testify. He felt that nobody should be punished for what happened. The lieutenant was a nice guy, doing a tough job in the heat. I agreed for a different reason. I believed that a month or two later, a final appeal review by the Naval Board of Records in Washington would find that the Law Officer had erred. For that reason, I felt that Woodley could only make it worse for himself if he testified again[5].

A month or so later, the lieutenant was tried at Phu Bai. I did not attend the trial and Woodley did not testify against him. The lieutenant was found 'not guilty.' Both Woodley and the lieutenant were functioning in extreme heat and exhaustion. In my experience, one's ability to think abstractly is seriously compromised, especially after casualties in the jungle and being tired and weak. These men are heroes. They need to be judged with the understanding of what they had faced. There was a lesson to be learned here.

---

5 After I was released from active duty late in December of 1967, as a civilian I visited Woodley in Portsmouth N.H. Naval Prison. With Woodley's permission, I contacted an attorney in Washington DC, who then freely represented Woodley before the Naval Board of Records. End result, the sentence was reduced to two years and a Bad Conduct Discharge.

FOURTEEN

LUNCHEON SURPRISE

On one of my trips North to Dong Ha, I was scheduled to examine two witnesses in preparation for a forthcoming trial. The two Marines were in a tent, and I joined them. They looked alert and intelligent. I began by asking general background questions. The witnesses would be OK. When it became time to get down to the facts and details, it was the lunch period. It would be nice to get out of the hot tent. "I'll see you in thirty minutes, and we should be able to wind this up today."

I walked about fifty yards away to the Officers Mess Hall which was a large tent with tables and chairs.

There was a long serving table with deep aluminum trays which contained a variety of foods. The lunch was one of my favorites,

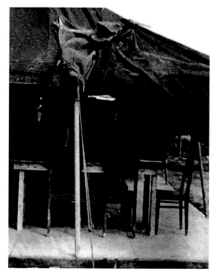

spaghetti and meatballs. I held my metal tray forward and the server dumped some food on my tray. I went back to my seat and began to enjoy my feast. Then I saw a little worm wiggling to get out of the hot tomato sauce. I gently removed the visitor with two fingers and flipped him out the side of the tent. The meal was too good to be ruined by a little worm. So, I just dug in with pleasure.

Soon, I felt a very strange feeling of a pulsing sensation in the air. It felt like a car pulled up behind you with huge base speakers going full blast. The vibration made you think you were having a heart attack . A few seconds later there were tremendous 'booms', and the pots and pans and dishes went flying off the table.

I instinctively rolled off my chair and 'hit the deck.' So did the others nearby. It was 'incoming' alright. I heard someone saying it was artillery, fired from North Vietnam over the DMZ and into this Marine forward position. Wow. I had not experienced incoming artillery before. After a few loud explosions, it ended. The group straightened up, took their trays, and refilled them if their food wasn't dumped out of the containers.

Lunch over, I then started walking back to the area where the witness tent was. I was a little disoriented, or so I thought, because I didn't see the tent. Someone saw me looking and said, "A direct hit. They were vaporized."

I stood still for a minute. Strangely, I didn't immediately feel the tragedy of two lives lost. My first thought was survival, distancing myself from the DMZ, and whether I could catch the last flight back to Phu Bai. I started jogging toward the airstrip. As I reached it, someone was walking back towards me and said, "You just missed it." To me, that meant another night on the DMZ, but then I saw a small two-engine non-military plane parked at the edge of the field, and a guy in a flight suit standing next to it. I approached the man and said, "Hey, any chance I could get a lift to Phu Bai?"

> The man replied, see those two plain clothed guys over there? I must sneak over to the North so they can parachute in tonight. Probably CIA. But it isn't quite dark enough. I'll go ask them. The crewman came back with a smile and said, sure Captain, we'll give you a lift.

Unbelievable luck, I thought. The plane held four people: Two pilots up front, and two places in the back. One for the crew chief and one for me. I was relieved that I would be sleeping in my own cot tonight. We took off. The plane was strikingly noisy. The three crew members had pilot's caps on with small microphones attached so they could communicate. All that was left for me was to look out the small window to my right. Once air bound, the sky to my right lit up like the 4th of July. Then, I looked closer and saw that it was pink streaks coming from the ground up and just missing the plane. We were the target of ground fire tracers. I immediately tapped the guy next to me and pointed out the window. The crew chief saw the display and then said a few words into his microphone. Quickly, the pilot shut off the plane's lights and veered down and to the left. We escaped.

A short while later, I was dropped off at the Phu Bai airstrip, and the unmarked civilian plane took off again. It was now after dark. As I walked through the empty airstrip terminal, I felt like James Bond as the few personnel stared at me. I was relieved to be home, to my hut, bed, and footlocker. I rubbed the "Chai."

FIFTEEN

BUFFALO DAY

One day, when I was the Perimeter Watch Officer again, I arrived early in an open sided Jeep with a driver. As we began to move around to inspect the perimeter, with the Jeep bumping up and down and the gears grinding, I thought I heard hooves and grunts coming my way. I turned my head to the right and saw a huge water buffalo charging toward the Jeep. As the driver pushed the Jeep as fast as it could go, the buffalo's trajectory suggested there would be a messy collision. While bouncing up and down in my seat, I fumbled to get my hand on the .45 in my hip holster. While still bouncing, with the buffalo closing in on us, I managed to get the ammunition clip into the pistol and cock it. Then, I tried to aim between the running buffalo's eyes. At that moment, the ground leveled out, the Jeep began to gain speed, and we were able to pull away from an imminent disaster (and a possible Foreign Claim for the death of someone's water buffalo). By the time we came back to the area, all was quiet, and I was dropped off at my underground bunker.

Shortly thereafter, the Marines arrived. I instructed them while in the bleachers, and the evening of securing the base began. After dark, I had only one buzz from a foxhole. A Marine on the perimeter thought he saw a cigarette butt outside the wire. I told him he could put it out with three shots, which were taken immediately. There were no more sightings.

It was a quiet night until a different one of my radios buzzed. I picked up the microphone and answered, "Perimeter Watch, Captain Zonderman." An authoritative HQ voice stated, "Be advised that a large Viet Cong force is heading toward your position and is about a kilometer away." I just said, "Yes, Sir." My first thought was, "What is a nice boy like me doing in a place like this?" My second thought was to prepare. I called in the sergeant of the Reserve Platoon, shared the message, and told to him to get his people ready. "If there is a break in our perimeter, I will send you there to fill it. Spread the word."

The next few hours were a bit tense, but thankfully quiet. It was a pleasant sight to see the sun rise. I wondered if that shot at the cigarette butt showed our alertness and discouraged a possible attack. The Marines were trucked out, and I made a quick trip to the Mess Hall.

SIXTEEN

THE BARDACK TRIAL

The next morning in the Division Legal Quonset hut, I was assigned as Defense Counsel in another murder case. Pvt. John Bardack was the defendant. I participated in the Article 32 investigation at Phu Bai where it would be determined whether there was sufficient cause to charge the person and then move the matter to Court Martial.

In the 130-degree heat, Pvt. Bardack was directing military traffic at one of the gates of the Phu Bai base camp. He brought with him three chilled cans of Coke to help him get through the day. They were his treasure.

Along came a Vietnamese boy about 12 and asked Bardack if he wanted some "boom-boom", a reference for sex and usually by his sister. He said "no" and told the boy to get away. The boy then offered to sell marijuana to him. The Marine's answer was the same, "Get out of here." As a truck came to the gate, Bardack walked away to check in the truck. The young boy then used this opportunity to steal Bardack's Cokes and run away. When Bardack discovered the theft, he yelled to the boy to bring his Coke back. The boy kept running. When he was about 100 yards away, feeling safe, he stopped, turned, and laughed at Bardack. The furious Marine picked up his rifle and took a single shot which killed the boy.

There was no doubt about who killed the boy. Nevertheless, an Article 32 investigative hearing was required. In the tent, present were the Hearing Officer, Lt. Colonel Cotton, the accused John Bardack, the boy's father, name unknown, and I was serving as the

Defense Counsel. Bardack sat next to me, both facing Colonel Cotton, and the father was seated on the left side. After the preliminaries, I noticed that Bardack was not nervous or afraid, and had a pleasant smile on his face. Then, a few minutes later, the boy's father took out a cigarette. Bardack jumped up, flicked his lighter on, went over to the father, lit his cigarette, and came back to his seat with a smile on his face. He was enjoying this murder trial pre-hearing as if it were about someone else. At this point, I said to the colonel, "Sir, I'd like to move that we adjourn this hearing to have the defendant mentally examined by the proper medical authority." The motion was granted, and the hearing was adjourned.

The first Naval doctor to examine Bardack was in Danang. He found that the defendant was exhibiting mental illness, a possible defense. Sometime later, a second doctor examined him at Yokosuka Naval Hospital in Japan. He also found that Bardack was mentally unfit to stand trial.

I was made aware of these findings. The command persisted, and Bardack was next sent to a stateside Naval Hospital in Philadelphia. Now, far away from the war, in an air-conditioned office, this third doctor said, "He's OK. Send him back to Vietnam for trial."

I was notified. As Bardack's counsel, it was obvious to me to request the first two doctors as witnesses in any forthcoming trial. I spoke to the Division Legal Officer, Colonel Flannigan and made the request.

One night when I was alone in the office reviewing some documents, I answered the phone. It was Colonel Flannigan, obviously drunk, and furious about my request for the first two doctors. The colonel yelled:

> These doctors were Navy Reservists who had served their time and were now civilians in private practice. You are causing us to restore them to active duty and bring them here at great cost. I am going to notify the Massachusetts Bar Association and have you disbarred.

What a frightening situation, to be in a hostile, primitive country, in the middle of a war, and have the man who controls you hate you and threaten you[6]. A chill went through me. After that, Flannigan made no further mention of this conversation, and I hoped it was a drunken one which he would not remember. Nevertheless, I had a moral decision to make. The next day, I put my request officially in writing, and additionally requested a more senior officer to assist me due to the unusual circumstances. I was removed from the case thereafter. However, the two doctors were brought from stateside, and the case was assigned to another attorney in the group, one who later made a career of the Marine Corps. Bardack was ultimately found guilty and sentenced to prison. The conviction was later reviewed in Washington D.C. The case against Bardack was dismissed based upon the psychiatric evidence that I had insisted be included in the record.

By now, I heard that Gus Anderson, after being transferred out, had been awarded a "Meritorious Service Medal", as did the previous Foreign Claims Officers, because of a dangerous **additional** job well done. I correctly predicted that I would not be so nominated for this award by my colonel because of my ethical choices in the Bardack case. I was happy for the tall, skinny, light haired private who had already spent some time in prison. He was now free to go back to his family and obtain counseling, as needed.

---

6 10 U.S.C. § 837, art. 37 prohibits such conduct.

SEVENTEEN

FAREWELL TO WAR

As I faced the last two months in Vietnam, I was finally a 'salty' short timer. My total service obligation would be satisfied when I came home from Asia. I could feel the magnetic pull of going home, being a husband, father, son, and practicing law. Nevertheless, I continued with my regular duties. There were other trials and Foreign Claims to be resolved. There were more trips North. I still filled my weekly chart of squares showing each colored-in week that I was in Vietnam, and each uncolored square which showed time remaining. One look at your scorecard and you could count the days until you flew away in the big bird.

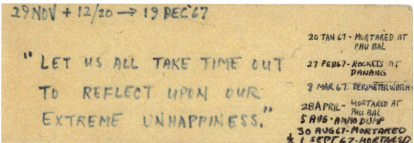

As the uncolored squares became fewer and fewer, my departure became more urgent, and I became more hypervigilant. It came with the territory. As others came within a week or two, they allowed themselves to think of home and family, and each passing day became the conscious attempt to stay alive.

One day when I was in Danang, I happened upon a ceremony honoring the 3rd Marine Division with a Presidential Unit Citation (PUC). Vice President Hubert Humphrey was pinning a special striper on the 3dMarDiv flag. This was a tremendous honor given to the Division for:

> "Extraordinary heroism in action against an armed enemy . . . which set it apart from and above other units participating in the same campaign. . . . The degree of heroism required is the same as that which would be required for award of the Navy Cross to an individual." (excerpt)

This citation included all units of our Division, including Headquarters Battalion. It authorized its members in country during the period from 3/8/65 to 9/15/67 to wear the Presidential Unit Citation medal.

The time finally came to leave this place and return to the other side of the world. My first flight outbound was the C-130 from Phu Bai to Danang. The second C-130 flight was from Danang to Okinawa, where I picked up my green uniform stored there. The flights to and from Phu Bai and Danang, all bore the risk of ground fire. I could relax only when I was up in the clouds on the way to Okinawa. I breathed a sigh of relief when I was finally out of range of ground fire. The plane out of Okinawa was a beautiful large commercial jet.

Once on that plane, I felt completely safe for the first time. I was heading home. I was a free man with a wife and child waiting for me. My memory of the long flight to California is vague. After we landed, I spent several days being examined and tested in a California Naval Hospital. For me, this was a discharge physical. How nice.

The commercial flight from California to Boston required a change of planes in Chicago, transferring to a flight to Boston's Logan airport. The stop-over brought me into the Chicago terminal. Proudly wearing my Marine Corps greens for the first time in a year, I noticed that walking through the airport, there were no smiles or waives. There was no "thank you for your service." Many people either lowered their eyes to the floor or glanced at me with disapproval. I was not previously aware of the extent of stateside anti-Vietnam sentiment. Resuming life back in the U.S. would have some adjustments.

On the last lap of the trip, I let myself think about who would be meeting me? My wife, parents, and Ann's sister, Bette. Ann's mother remained at our new home with Lauren. Ann's decision was for me to meet Lauren the next morning in the privacy of our home, just mom, dad, and baby.

Inside Logan airport, there they were. The people who worried about me every day. I handed the "Chai" back to my mother. Nothing needed to be said. I was home, I was safe. I hugged Ann and held onto her. Then handshakes and kisses for my parents, and a hug and kiss for Bette.

The first stop was my parent's home, where many family members had gathered. Everybody around me was happy and loving, laughter abounded. We talked actively, feeling the joy in each other's presence, now gratefully including me. The dining room table was covered with my favorite foods . It was a cold, snowy winter night and the fire in the fireplace burned brightly.

I didn't mind the snow. I hadn't seen it in a year. The chilly, damp, wet days were behind me. The days ahead might not be easy, but as I looked at my loving, bright, caring, family, I recalled the motto of *"Omnia mea mecum porto."* I am the summation of these people, I thought. I will go forward with strength and resolve.

Ann had rented our new home. It was the first floor of a two-family house in Newton, near where I went to High School. She had outfitted it with furniture and everything else a normal house required. She was amazing. She did all this. I had not seen a television set or a Red Sox game in a year.

We didn't stay around my parents' home too long. I was anxious to see Lauren and where we would be living. When we arrived at our home, Lauren was sound asleep, but I lifted her out of her crib and gently held her against me, seeing, feeling, and smelling her for the first time, my seven-month-old daughter. The next morning, we would all happily crawl around together on the floor: Lauren, mom, dad, and Snuffy our dog.

We went to bed early and woke up early the next morning. I walked into Lauren's room . She was standing up in her crib. She was beautiful. She had big blue eyes like her mother and a beautiful smile. I lifted her out of her crib and tickled her, hearing her voice for the first time. Later that day we went out in the snow and pulled her around on her sled. Words can't describe this moment of my life. With Ann and Lauren by my side, 1968 would be a very happy New Year.

Then along came our son Jeffrey, in 1969. I was joyfully there for his birth on November 28th.

EIGHTEEN

WHO AM I?

After returning from Vietnam (12/1967), close friends often asked how the experience changed me. I began to think about that question over time. My initial reaction was for the worse. It took away my presumption of human sanity and my presumption of human indestructability. It changed my outlook on humanity and safety. It showed how cruel and unfeeling that we human beings could be to each other. It showed how easily we could engage in and endure violence. It showed how vulnerable the human body was, and that young people would not necessarily live long lives. The result was more than just philosophical. These are presumptions that let us live our lives calmy and confidently.

Vietnam veterans tend to be hypervigilant. It isn't temporary. It has lasted me all my life. It reminds me of my grandmother who used to yell, "Be careful Paulie, its slippery out." When you have to think about every step you take, or what's happening around the corner, because the unexpected can snuff out your life in a second, you don't become afraid, but you become extra careful. Your memory establishes hyper vigilance. I realize that I am like that; but of course, I'm a grandfather now, and that's the way I'm expected to be. Things can come from a grandparent's experience or can come from a young man's experience who has seen the dark side of humanity. You get hardened to it. Except, in my case, I learned early and lived with it. Recall when the trans-DMZ artillery wiped out my witness tent. I was told the men were vaporized from a direct hit. When you witness such a tragedy, you don't have the time to emote. It means acting decisively to protect yourself. You don't have time to be shocked or to mourn. You are motivated by hyper-vigilance. In this case, I headed right for the airstrip.

People have recognized the Vietnam veterans by the "thousand-yard stare." You might call it a stone face. My wife often tells me to smile. It makes me use strange muscles, but I am getting better at it. We learned to control our emotions, and that can be a good thing in a war zone. In a friendly peaceful society, you are encouraged to show your feelings, to be polite. "How nice you look today." But combat veterans are not usually good "B.S.'ers." When somebody yells "incoming," you just react, and your life depends on it.

As my relatives and friends, you would agree that I'm a civilized person. Yet I find myself always aware of the dark side, especially in occasional dreams. Ever since the time I came home, I have maintained the right to carry a concealed weapon. I have made shooting a hobby and belong to a local gun club. I don't shoot often, but during my last few years as a judge, I wore a handgun under my robes. So did the other judge. I had to argue for a metal detector in the courtroom, and two police officers, one in the front and one in the back. Was that hypervigilant or just being careful? The other judge was not a veteran, but he wanted the same safeguards.

I have always been proud of being a Marine. The saying is "Once a Marine, always a Marine." It's true. As senior citizens, we are still proud. The training was challenging. "Run until somebody passes out." What a great way to build endurance. The combat assignments were dangerous, more so for others in the field. Nevertheless, I believe I have used up seven of my nine lives since being a teenager.

I feel warmly toward Vietnam veterans. I still practice the ritual when I see another Vietnam veteran. We say, "Welcome home brother" and shake hands. That is the cure for not being welcomed by the public at large.

I believe veterans wish to care for one another. When on the bench and presented with veterans who were acting out, I tried to refer them to the Veteran's Administration for care or counsel. I have belonged to veterans' organizations as long as I can remember.

I guess my ethics and morality were tested by my commanders in the Court Martial situations, and I'll never know the consequences in my records since I did not elect to make the Marines a career. I stand by my ethical and professional decisions. The Marines have now created a Judge Advocate Department, so the lawyers answer only to other lawyers higher in the command structure. There should be no more command pressure put on the trial lawyer. The federal statutes now prohibit it in detail.

All this is jumbled together in answering the opening question. I have great pride in my service. The officer training taught leadership and a 'never give up' spirit.

At the same time, I am angry and disappointed with our government who sent us on a fool's mission, from which 58,000 of us didn't return. I am disappointed with a government which didn't provide us with jungle clothing and boots, and promptly even with a handgun. I am mostly angry with our government who 'betrayed us and sprayed us' with Agent Orange even after they knew that dioxin was a terribly strong and long-lasting poison. They took unwarranted risks with our lives. My trust in government and politics is severely tarnished.

After all of this, in 2003, I was diagnosed with Leukemia (CLL), blood cancer, an Agent Orange presumptive illness. I thought I had made it home safely thirty-six years before. The medical books told me, at age 64, that I had a 50% chance to live five years. That was a real punch in the stomach. The Marines always taught us that you react to being ambushed, by turning into the ambush and charging. I then began to do some research on CLL. I found a Mayo Clinic protocol which said that green tea capsules had been successful in controlling CLL. Since then, every day of my life, I have taken a green tea capsule (called EGCG) and it seems to have caused a remission in the problem. It certainly worried me, but I put it aside and just concentrated on my new job (2002) as a Town Judge, and successfully served twelve years, frequently being called out at 3:00 am to arraign someone. I am pleased to say that my reputation was as "being fair." At least the police thought so. Looking back, all I can say is that the military experience changed me in many negative ways, but I still wake up in the morning with pride and look forward to a good life with my wife, family and friends.

EPILOG

Let me begin with the thought that the Vietnam war was a waste of time and lives. I guess we all know that now. My heart goes out to the parents of the young men and women who didn't make it home. They answered the call. They had faith in their government.

Vietnam War Memorial, Washington D.C.

Unfortunately, we never learned our lesson. We still send troops into far off lands to make wars which can't be won, or victories that disappear as soon as we leave. Vietnam didn't teach our leaders anything.

There are many books on the Vietnam war that are critical. In my opinion, the best and most intelligent comment that sums the war up in a small paragraph is in Tim O'Brien's recent book, "Dad's Maybe Book."[7]

> "I hated the place. I hated myself for being there. Beyond that, as a purely practical problem, we were caught up in a confusing and deadly civil struggle. No front, no rear, no clear battle lines, no military purpose, no way to distinguish friend from foe. The enemy was everywhere and nowhere, vanishing into tunnels and popping up behind us and then sliding away again. We didn't know the language. We didn't know the culture. We didn't know where we were at any given time or why we were there."

---

7 First Mariner Books Edition 2020, Houghton Mifflin Harcourt, Boston and NY, copyright c 2019 by Tim O'Brien, page 201.

I have been planting flags on veterans' graves for several years. In this picture, my two granddaughters are helping me. I hope to develop a sense of patriotism in them. This is even though as I go to publication, the US has withdrawn from Afghanistan after a twenty-year presence. The comparison to our futile history in Vietnam is compelling/sobering. Our government doesn't learn from their mistakes, at the expense of veterans' lives.

AGENT ORANGE

There is another aspect of Vietnam that doesn't get enough attention, and that is Agent Orange (2,4-D + 2,4,5-T), a Dow chemical product. The 2,4,5-T contained 'dioxin'. It was a deadly substance that was sprayed by aircraft onto the forest (and troops) in Vietnam from 1962-1970. Its purpose was to kill the foliage around military bases so that any approaching enemy would be out in the open. Unknown to us, it was in the air we breathed and on our skin. Unfortunately, dioxin can kill or disable anyone exposed to it; and we are learning that it can be passed through DNA to the children of Vietnam Veterans. What a heartbreak it is for a disabled veteran to learn that he has brought disability or deformity home to his newly born children.

Agent Orange attacks the body in several ways, sometimes quickly and other times many years later. People have come down with illnesses on the VA list of 'presumptive diseases' as many as 35+ years after leaving Vietnam. Dioxin has an alleged half-life of over one million years. It is known as the deadliest chemical agent. If a veteran has a serious illness later in life, long after leaving Vietnam, he/she should check the VA's 'presumptive list' of illnesses it causes. Too many veterans have ignored their rights and died without getting the VA free care as well as disability compensation.

The US government estimates that as many as 2.4 million service members were exposed to Agent Orange. The US troops had left Vietnam in 1975, when the communists took over the country.

Congress, for the first time in 1991, sixteen years later, approved Agent Orange compensation for Vietnam Veterans with only two diseases: non-Hodgkin's Lymphoma and Soft Tissue Sarcoma. (It is also important to note the terrible impact of Agent Orange on the Vietnamese people, and their land and waterways.) It was a tough battle to add the many other diseases now attributed to Agent Orange, but the 'Vietnam Veterans of America' kept up the fight. Today, the following are treated as presumptively caused by Agent Orange without further evidence, if you spent military time in Vietnam. Once you are approved, various levels of VA disability compensation and treatment are available. Below is the current list of presumptive diseases:

> AL Amyloidosis, Asthma, Bladder Cancer, Chronic B-cell Leukemias, Chloracne, Diabetes Mellitus Type 2, Hodgkin's Disease, Hypothyroidism, Ischemic Heart Disease, Multiple Myeloma, Non-Hodgkin's Lymphoma, Parkinsonism, Parkinson's Disease, Peripheral Neuropathy, Porphyria Cutanea Tarda, Prostate Cancer, Respiratory Cancers, Rhinitis, Sinusitis, Soft Tissue Sarcomas (other than osteosarcoma, chondrosarcoma, Kaposi's sarcoma, or Mesothelioma.[8]

A class action lawsuit was brought by Vietnam Veterans and their families in 1984 because of their exposure to Agent Orange used during the Vietnam War. The suit was brought against the major manufacturers of these herbicides. The class action case was settled out-of-court in 1984 for $180 million dollars, reportedly the largest settlement of its kind at that time. The closing date for submitting claims into this fund was December 31, 1994, ten years later.

---

8 This is the VA list of the "presumptive diseases" thru September of 2021.

I had not been diagnosed until 2003. I thus joined a second Class-Action like the first. The federal appeals judge in New York threw out our class action saying that the defendants were released from liability by the first case. How can you sue if you are not sick yet? I think the federal government still wanted to avoid this issue.

I thought I had put the Agent Orange fiasco behind me, but then I viewed the 90-minute video film cited below. It infuriated me that our government, as of 2015, was still allowing the Agent Orange to be sprayed in the Pacific Northwest to defoliate for the lumber industry. The courts and agencies have continued to cover it up.

If you are interested in how Agent Orange was created and why was it used, you should view the below disc from PBS. It lays out amazing facts that are largely unknown. On the following pages are the major points of the documentary.[9]

---

9 "The People vs. Agent Orange," a disk video documentary produced by PBS and aired in 2021. c2020 Films for Humanity, Inc. and Arte France. Produced and Directed by Alan Adelson and Kate Taverna.
See YouTube/The People vs. Agent Orange.
https://shop.pbs.org/WD5922DV.ht

"THE PEOPLE VS. AGENT ORANGE"

CAROL VAN STRUM, ENVIRONMENTALIST AND AUTHOR PBS DOCUMENTARY

> *"In its own way, Agent Orange was the most destructive incidence of chemical warfare in our history."*

- In December 1960, Communism was on the rise during the Kennedy administration. Kennedy wanted to stop it where it was. He loved the idea that American ingenuity, not just bombs, but more surgical technologies, could be used to defeat these insurgencies.

- The revolutionary chemical 2-4-D Agent Orange was part of that strategic view.

- Dow chemical had developed the 2-4-D weed killer.

- Saigon government in 1961 was a vigorous proponent of herbicides in Vietnam.

- In October 1961, President Diem was begging the US to spray his trees. He wanted urgent action to deliver 2-4-D to Vietnam.

- There was confusion in Washington whether to use 2-4-D Agent Orange. It was resolved that as long as the spraying was controlled, the Geneva Conference was not being violated. It would not be chemical warfare as long as it was not sprayed on people, but to defoliate.

- Nov. 30, 1961. The White house, in a Top-Secret Communication: NSA 2115, approved a selective and carefully controlled joint program of defoliant and cooperation in Vietnam.

- McGeorge Bundy (National Security Advisor under Presidents Kennedy and Johnson 1961-66), believed one goal was denial for the Communists: take away the forest cover, take away the insurgents' ability to hide and conduct guerilla operations.

- But, once the overall war escalated, the defoliation program followed right behind it. *"Spraying millions of gallons of highly concentrated herbicide indiscriminately over a vast area of forest many times over was highly destructive and massive. It was a weapon of mass destruction."*

- From 1962-1971, Operation Ranch Hand was the name of the herbicide program run by the US Air Force in Vietnam.

- The federal government nationalized all the chemical companies to produce only Agent Orange for Vietnam. The chemical companies knew that the more they produced, the more money they would make. They violated the industry standards to produce herbicides by using a process much quicker with higher temperatures which resulted in the production of dioxin in the finished product. They knew it posed risks to the people and the land, and that the effects could be devastating.

- Dow's response to the government: we cannot produce the amount you want and maintain low levels of dioxin being in the finished product. The government said, "Don't worry about it. We need it for the jungle. And if it happens to get into it, we're at war." They knew dioxin was an extremely potent carcinogenic, mutagenic, and trajectogenic … very potent agent.

- Vietnam – 1966: "I saw the plane spraying, was drenched in it…I didn't know that powder was poisoning me" (a serviceman speaking).

- Vietnam 1971: Captain Clary, US Air force, did a comprehensive study on Agent Orange. He determined that there were indications that there were some real problems for people exposed to Agent Orange. He was ordered to dump/erase computers used in SE Asia including Laos. The report was immediately classified Top Secret. The government kept it locked up for over 35 years and denied that any of it existed.

- The US government halted the use of Agent Orange in Vietnam in 1971, ending the decade long herbicidal war.

- Senator Thomas Daschle, Senate Majority Leader, 2001, stated the government's action was tantamount to a cover-up…There was information that was withheld and distortions that were commonplace, that did a real disservice to the veterans and our rule of law. "All of that occurred with far greater regularity than I would like to acknowledge."

- BUT USE IN AMERICAN FORESTS AND RANGE LANDS, allegedly 'removed from human contact', is allowed to continue TODAY.

- Lincoln County, Oregon, 2015, was being sprayed over watersheds (drinking water) to defoliate trees for the lumber industry there, the day that the PBS documentary was being filmed. The Forest Service was unwilling to do any fact finding about the effect of the spraying. The consequences include miscarriages within a month of spraying, multiple reports of injury and death to people and animals in the region, which have all been covered up. They deny the effect of dioxin.

- Citizens Against Toxic Sprays in Lincoln County filed a court action. The chemical companies denied the consequences; and local people were intimidated, threatened, and evidence made to disappear.

NEGATIVE POPULARITY

The war in Vietnam was very unpopular in the United States, and so were the American soldiers who participated. Only recently has the public softened its comments from "baby killer" to "thank you for your service." President Jimmy Carter made a Proclamation as far back as 1979 creating a 'Vietnam Veterans Week'.

> "The decade now drawing to a close began in the midst of a war that was the **longest and most expensive in our history, and most costly in human lives and suffering.** Because it was a divisive and painful period for all Americans, we are tempted to put the Vietnam war out of our minds. But it is important that we remember - - honestly, realistically, with humility.
>
> It is important, too, that we remember those who answered their Nation's call in that war with the full measure of valor and loyalty, that we pay full tribute at last to all Americans who served in our armed forces in Southeast Asia. Their courage and sacrifices in that tragic conflict were made doubly difficult by the Nation's lack of agreement as to what constituted the highest duty. Instead of glory, they were too often met with our embarrassment or ignored when they returned. (emphasis added)
>
> The honor of those who died there is not tarnished by our uncertainty at the moment of their sacrifice. To them we offer our respect and gratitude. …**To those who still bear the wounds, both physical and psychic, from all our wars, we acknowledge our continuing responsibility.**"

Only recently, has the younger public thanked us for our service. The government has never created an award like the Purple Heart for the veterans who died or became disabled by Agent Orange in a combat zone. There was once a movement to establish a "Silver Rose" medal for the Agent Orange victims. This is on the congressional record somewhere but has been a dead issue.

11/11/2014

Thank you "Dad, Poppy, Paul, for serving our country as a Captain in the U.S.A. Marine Corps in the Vietnam War. We are very proud of you. We can't believe you survived!

In your honor we are having your name engraved on a plaque to be mounted at Ammunition Hill in Jerusalem Israel, with other brave soldiers from around the world.

Kyra   We love you   Laure
CLAiRE   Bella
Booper-Ann   Jeff